MENDING
the
NETS

MENDING
the
NETS

TWO VISIONS ONE PASSION

The Restoration of God's People

PATRICK CHAMBRON

Sovereign World

Published by Sovereign World Ltd
Ellel Grange
Bay Horse
Lancaster
Lancashire LA2 0HN
United Kingdom

www.sovereignworld.com

Originally published in French under the title *"Ellel Ministries France, Deux visions une même passion, La restauration du people de Dieu"* by Éditions Ellel Ministries France,10, Avenue Jules Ferry, 38380 Saint-Laurent-du-Pont.

Translation by Shirley Ansell. Edited by David Cross.

ISBN: 978-1-85240-854-1
E-book: 978-1-85240-857-2

Typesetting and cover design by Graeme Andrew

Printed in Great Britain by Bell and Bain Ltd, Glasgow

Patrick and Valerie, you say in your heart, "I want to throw out the net." The Lord says, "Yes, but I am going to put new tools into your hands. There are nets you must repair and I, the Lord, will put these new tools into your hands, and I am going to teach you how to repair the nets. The Lord will bring to you many people whom you are going to train in how to repair nets."

Contents

Preface to the French edition

For servants of God, gifted with a shepherd's heart, the desire to see restoration in the lives of those under their care will burn with a passion as strong as any other call within the Body of Christ. Such a passion took on a special dimension in the lives of Patrick and Valerie Chambron.

In the story described in this book, we discover how God sowed a vision for restoration of His people into the heart of an apostolic leader called Peter Truschel. He then recognised how that vision was to be fulfilled through Patrick and Valerie. In the Body of Christ, the restoration of lives, torn apart by the sinfulness of this world and defiled by the work of the enemy, is an essential work for bringing about the fulfilment of God's purposes on earth.

It's amazing to see how God leads the footsteps of those whom He has called into such a ministry, in a way that connects them with others who have been called into the same work. This book describes such a meeting between Ellel Ministries and Patrick and Valerie, a connection that was to significantly strengthen this couple in their call to bring the ministry of restoration to the church in France. Patrick and Valerie discovered in Ellel Ministries men and women also passionate for the spiritual health of all those in the Body of Christ. The meeting of these two visions also resulted in Patrick discovering a treasure trove of precious principles important for the healing ministry.

The relationship that God arranged with Peter and Fiona Horrobin, founders of Ellel Ministries, and with their colleagues David and Denise Cross, clarified the calling that was already in the hearts of Patrick and Valerie. The result was to be not just of benefit to these two servants of God, nor just to the church that they were pastoring, but to all those involved in pastoral care in the church in France.

I am personally grateful for all that we have received through faithful and obedient men and women, led by the Holy Spirit, but I am particularly grateful to Patrick for his perseverance in seeking to share, not least to the rising generation, the precious tools he has learned, for the heaing of this broken world.

Christian Rivière
(former president of the group of Evangelical
Pentecostal Churches, based in Grenoble)

Introduction to the English edition

Patrick Chambron is the Centre Director for the work of Ellel Ministries in France and is also taking on the role of Regional Director for the centres in Western Europe. In 2009 (updated in 2015) he wrote about his amazing journey with God in becoming involved, along with his wife Valerie, in the ministry of restoration for the Body of Christ in France.

It is a story of the meeting of two visions. One was received through the Senior Pastor Pierre Truschel and given to Patrick while he was working as a full-time pastor in a church at St Laurent du Pont in France, and the other was given to Peter Horrobin, the founder of Ellel Ministries, a healing ministry based near Lancaster in England. As Patrick's walk with the Lord progressed, it became evident that it was His plan to bring the healing and deliverance ministry into France in a new way. It would be through Patrick's unexpected connections with Ellel Ministries and the establishing of that ministry at the Christian Fraternity in St Laurent du Pont.

I have known Patrick and Valerie for nearly twenty years and I have been impressed by their integrity and perseverance. Moreover, I have had the privilege of witnessing their unfolding story of discovering God's plan for their lives. Some years ago, Shirley Ansell, then a member of the ministry team at the Ellel centre of Glyndley Manor, was encouraged to translate Patrick's book. When I came across this translation recently, I felt strongly prompted by the Lord to make the story available to English-speaking readers, as another precious record of the way God has His hand on people's lives, and how He wonderfully brings His people together for His purposes.

In this book, Patrick first gives us a brief history of Peter Horrobin and the founding of Ellel Ministries. He then shares a comprehensive description of his own background and his journey with God, and the story of how Ellel became established in France. In the last two chapters, Patrick describes a significant prophetic revelation of torn fishing nets and his fervent belief in the need for restoration of broken lives in the Body of Christ, in preparation for an end-times harvest of souls.

I trust that God will encourage you through the pages of this book.

David Cross, September 2021

CHAPTER 1

The history and vision of Ellel Ministries International

How Ellel Ministries started

Peter Horrobin, the founder and international director of Ellel Ministries, was born in 1943 in Bolton, Lancashire, England. His ancestors were Huguenots who had fled from France in the seventeenth century to take refuge in South Africa. Peter was born into a Christian family and had a personal relationship with Jesus Christ even as a small child. At the age of eleven, he became aware of God's call on his life and was baptised by total immersion at the age of sixteen.

Having gained the required qualifications at school, he went to the University of Oxford where he studied chemistry and chemical microbiology. Following Oxford, he spent five years lecturing on Building Science and

Technology, first at Oxford Polytechnic and then Manchester University.

Peter has always had a keen interest in classic cars and he has written several books on the subject. One day he managed to buy a very damaged version of one of his favourite cars and set to work on its restoration. Having fully dismantled the car, he sadly realised that it had a severely bent chassis, but in that moment he heard God say to him, "Yes, you are capable of fully restoring the chassis of this old car, but I can restore the lives of people who are deeply broken." And then later Peter heard God speaking to him and asking, "Are you willing to spend the rest of your life bringing healing to those in need, and teaching others to do the same?"

For sixteen years Peter prayed, alongside others, into the vision he had been given. Then in 1985, at a conference led by John Wimber in Sheffield, he experienced an overwhelming sense of God's love and felt Him speaking three specific words: accepted, restored and commissioned. In the autumn of the same year, while Peter was searching for a suitable location for the healing centre that he felt God wanted him to establish, an estate agent friend suggested he visit a property called Ellel Grange, just as an example of what might be suitable. In fact, the house was not for sale but when Peter visited, the Lord clearly said, "This is the place, claim it for Me!" At that time the house was fully operational as a residential health establishment and, despite Peter's enquiries, the owners confirmed that the property was definitely not on the market.

Still convinced that God had spoken to him about this property, Peter left a business card in case they changed their minds and, three months later, he received a telephone call asking him if he was still interested in purchasing the house. Peter replied that he was indeed interested, but he knew in his heart that there was a big problem. He had no money. If the purchase was to take place, obtaining sufficient finance would truly take a miracle.

A noteworthy, if somewhat humorous confirmation of God's hand on the property, came from an unexpected source. For some time, Peter had been blessed by the prayers of a faithful woman of God, an Irish nun by the name of Sister Aine. One day when they were reflecting on the fact that Ellel Grange was located just off exit 33 of the M6 motorway, Sister Aine remarked that it was at the age of 33 that Jesus exited from His earthly ministry!

Through many amazing gifts and loans, the necessary finance did indeed miraculously come together. On 31 October 1986, there were sufficient funds to purchase the Ellel Grange estate, with just a few pounds to spare, enough in fact to cover a small celebration! Peter and his friends then set about praying over the house and the whole estate, seeking God's cleansing of the ground and buildings, and they consecrated it all for the purposes of God. The first Healing Retreat for guests took place at Ellel Grange in January 1987.

Over the following years it became apparent that God was calling Ellel Ministries to pursue the purchase of other centres both in the UK and around the world.

The centres in England included Glyndley Manor near the south coast and Pierrepont on the outskirts of London. Today the Ministry has more than thirty centres of activity worldwide.

The vision, mission and name of Ellel Ministries

As the work became established, there was a need to make a clear statement of the purposes of Ellel Ministries, in line with what Peter believed God had revealed to him. The vision and mission statements for the work, based on Luke 9:11 and Isaiah 61:1-7, were summerised as follows:

> *Ellel Ministries is a non-denominational Christian mission organisation with a vision to resource and equip the Church by welcoming people, teaching them about the Kingdom of God, and healing those in need.*

> *Its mission is to fulfil the above vision throughout the world, as God opens doors, in accordance with the great commission of Jesus, and the calling of the Church to proclaim the Kingdom of God by preaching the Good News, healing the broken-hearted and setting the captives free.*

The Ministry took its name from the first centre in Lancaster, at Ellel Grange. Interestingly the name *Ellel* is derived from an old English greeting *All Hail*. Friends of the Ministry in Israel have said that the nearest Hebrew translation of the word *Ellel* would be *towards God*, and the word apparently also sounds like *love flowing outward* in the Chinese language. So, we could perhaps say that the name Ellel stands for *All hail, King Jesus! Your love flowing outward into a needy world.* This certainly seems very appropriate for a Christian healing ministry!

CHAPTER 2

My early journey with God

Background

I was born in 1959, during the years of economic boom in France after the War. My Christian parents came from the Ardéchois Plateau and from Chambron sur Lignon in the Loire valley. My paternal grandparents, Paul and Emilie, grew up in the Darbystes (Brethren) Assembly. On my mother's side, my grandfather, André, was born into the Reformed church and married my grandmother, Yvonne, who was also from the Darbystes background.

During the Second World War, my paternal grandfather spent six years in Germany as a prisoner of war, so my grandmother was left alone to bring up my father between the ages of four and ten. Like many other wartime children, my parents were deeply affected by the German occupation and its consequences.

During the industrial growth of the 1950s, they left

the Ardéchois Plateau. My father began a career as a miner, working in St Etienne, which was not far from where my mother was working in Valence. At this time of redevelopment in France, housing was scarce and they found it difficult to get lodgings. But my parents worked hard and managed to buy a small four-roomed house as their first home, near to the Paris-Marseille railway line. Unable to look after me while they were both working full time, my mother sent me to live with my maternal grandmother. My mother had tried to find someone locally, but this had not worked out well, so from the age of two until four I lived with, and was taught by, my grandparents, living about seventy miles from Valence.

My grandfather was an assistant conductor on the railways and rarely at home, so I remember more of my grandmother, a simple and modest woman with a deep faith. I recall her reading her Bible and encouraging my mother to do the same. When I was five years old my youngest sister was born and my mother stopped working, so I was able to return to my parents home in Valence.

Christian education and student days

Although my parents clearly had a deep respect for God, we never talked about spiritual issues at home and they very rarely mentioned their faith. However, I realised that there was a difference between our family and others in the neighbourhood who were mainly Catholic. I attended the Sunday school at the Brethren Assembly and I remember having to learn passages of scripture by heart, a task that I seemed very willing to do.

As I grew up, it was my mother who took a particular interest in my education, my father being always so busy at work. Despite a problem with shyness and even some anxiety, I did quite well in my studies. Going to church on Sundays increasingly became more of an obligation than a pleasure, but I continued in order to please my parents. Then, at the age of eleven, when I was on holiday with my grandparents, I clearly remember my grandmother declaring her belief that I was not saved. In fact, I somehow knew deep in my heart that, if Jesus were to return, He would not take me to be with Him. I was convinced that my destination was hell and I lived with this fear, not really knowing how to be saved. As I look back now, it seems obvious that the enemy was taking advantage of this time of doubt, accusing me and making me feel guilty.

I had many friends during my teenage years and spent most of my time with them, so they were really my second family. Although I sometimes made mistakes, I thank God that, on the whole, I kept the right side of the law. At sixteen, I was invited by some cousins to take part in a Christian youth camp at Sanary-sur-Mer in the Var. Deep inside I knew that I was different from them and that I wanted to be like them, but sadly no one at the camp gave me the opportunity to accept Jesus Christ as my Saviour.

Following my eighteenth birthday, I left the Valentinoise region to go and live in Besançon (in the Doubs) to go to a college of engineering. At this time of my life I only had two objectives: to be successful in my studies and to enjoy myself. Sadly, this involved unhelpful friendships, disco parties and the use of alcohol, but it is now clear to me that God was watching over my life, including protection from several serious accidents. However, at the age of twenty-four, despite receiving an engineering diploma, I was struggling with depression following the break-up of a romantic relationship.

Meeting with Jesus

When I began my professional career in the Lyonnaise region, the inner emptiness I felt became increasingly severe, to the point where I felt that my life really had no meaning. One Sunday evening I remember calling out to God, "God, if You created everything, if You truly exist, show Yourself to me, because I believe that I'm on a slippery slope." The following Tuesday, I received a letter from my cousin, the one who had invited me to the Christian youth camp. In the letter he was inviting me to attend some evening prayer meetings and Bible studies.

I had not seen this cousin for eight years, so I took this as God's clear answer to my prayers. I went to the meeting the following week and there I surrendered myself to the Lord. It was such a pivotal moment, a return to God and a time of deep repentance began in my life. Day after day I discovered my need of Him and I truly experienced His presence and faithfulness. As time went by, I went to various Christian conferences with the group of young believers who had been at the youth camp all those years before. At one of these conferences, when the evangelist Luis Palau was speaking, I clearly heard God call me and say that I was to follow Him.

Having met personally with Jesus, I returned to the Brethren Assembly where I had gone with my parents, now with a real desire to live a Christian life, but I soon realised that such a walk has its share of difficulties and trials. From the time of my conversion, I had lots of questions even though I knew I was saved. Unfortunately, no one seemed to be able to answer these questions, and the Bible teaching that I was receiving didn't seem to line up with the Word of God concerning spiritual gifting. I couldn't understand why there was this obvious discrepancy.

Meeting Pentecostals and searching for the Holy Spirit

For reasons of employment I had to leave the Lyonnaise region and move to Bourgoin-Jallieu in Isère. I was still having personal struggles from the things that had happened to me in my earlier life and then, one evening, having planned a visit to the cinema, I crossed an area of town where a tent had been erected with a banner announcing *Jesus Saviour, Jesus Healer, Jesus Deliverer*. I went in and found myself going forward for the prayer of salvation. Those leading the meeting laid hands on me and encouraged me to contact the church that was organising the outreach event.

I went home feeling fearful because I had been taught that the laying on of hands was dangerous and should not be practised. As a result, I didn't follow up the address that I had been given, continuing to attend the Christian group in Lyon where I had been going. Unfortunately, I still had doubts about my salvation, and it seemed that my Christian life was far from adequate. Twelve months later, I moved again for employment reasons, this time to work for a large organisation in the Grenoble area. As I was not married, I had plenty of time to attend various meetings when these were available, but I recognised that I was a Christian without connection to a local church. I was clearly searching and often went to a small group of non-charismatic Christians who were wanting to discover the gifts of the Holy Spirit.

One day I made my way to a university Bible group meeting on the St Martin d'Heres campus and to my surprise the evening speaker was the evangelist I had met at the Bourboin-Jallieu tent meeting. This coincidence really challenged me and then, several weeks later, a Christian friend took me to Sunday morning service at the Pentecostal church, Rue des 400 Couverts, Grenoble. This charismatic church was clearly very much alive and moving in the power of the Holy Spirit, although I have to admit that it was all a bit of a shock!

I was somewhat overwhelmed as I was not used to dynamic services where the Holy Spirit moved powerfully over the Body of Christ in prophecy and healing. Nevertheless, I persevered, attending weekly Bible study meetings where I found the teaching to be clearly inspired by the Holy Spirit. One evening I unexpectedly met up with the same evangelist from the tent meeting, and this further coincidence challenged me even more. It was at this time that I also met Pierre Truschel, the Senior Pastor from the Chandelier church in Grenoble. He was to have such a significant influence on my spiritual life.

In the midst of all this, I found it difficult seeing so many Christians exercising the gifts of the Spirit, such as speaking in tongues and prophecy, because these practices were so unfamiliar to me. Intellectually I understood that these experiences were mentioned in the Bible and they conformed to scripture, but I felt so totally out of my depth with this apparent life in the Spirit.

A first taste of deliverance and freedom in the Holy Spirit

I regularly attended the Chandelier church, and joined one of their house-groups. In the autumn of 1986, the Senior Pastor organised a week of fasting, prayer and Bible teaching. The theme for the week was Principles of Deliverance Ministry. I went to the meetings every evening and at the end of the week we had the opportunity to put into practice the things we had learnt. To my great surprise, it seemed to open a door on issues relating to my adolescent and student years, and I found myself experiencing powerful deliverance. I saw for the first time the reality of how a Christian could be controlled by demonic forces in any part of their life that was not under the spiritual authority of Jesus.

I realise now that God took me through this deliverance, a work of sanctification, to prepare me to receive baptism in the Holy Spirit, which took place a few months later. Following this I began to speak in tongues and experience the gift of prophecy, and all this deeply transformed my spiritual life. For the first time I was able to witness to others about my faith with confidence and without a sense of embarrassment. The words of scripture had become true for me.

> *But you will receive power when the Holy Spirit has come upon you; and you shall be My witnesses both in Jerusalem, and in all Judea and Samaria, and even to the remotest part of the earth.*

(Acts 1:8)

God's call

> *For we are His workmanship, created in Christ Jesus for good works, which God prepared beforehand so that we would walk in them.*

(Ephesians 2:10)

One evening in 1986 our cell-group leader invited a Bible school teacher to share the Word of God at the meeting. This man, who was mature in the faith and in his understanding of the Bible, also had a particular gift in words of knowledge through the Holy Spirit. While he was teaching, he suddenly stopped and began to prophesy. His words deeply touched my heart and I realised that he was speaking out details of my life, both past and present. He then said, "This brother is being called to awaken the sleeping sheaves. There are many sheaves of corn asleep in the harvest field and they are cold or crushed, in need of restoration."

I was overwhelmed by the presence of the Lord and, even though I didn't fully understand the significance of these words, I felt convinced that God had spoken very precisely to me. Having grown up in the Brethren Assembly, I had no idea what it meant to be called by God into ministry. Paul's letters to the Ephesians had never challenged me personally and the idea of being called to build up and minister to the Body of Christ was totally unfamiliar to me.

And He gave some as apostles, and some as prophets, and some as evangelists, and some as pastors and teachers.

(Ephesians 4:11)

Joy in sowing with a new helper

Whatever your hand finds to do, do it with all your might
(Ecclesiastes 9:10a)

At the time I was still unmarried. God had not yet led me to my future wife but, since my baptism in the Holy Spirit, a strong commitment burned within me to serve Him in everything that He showed me to do. I had the privilege of devoting my annual leave to mission trips to Africa and to Christian camps for young and adolescent children. As it turned out, I met Valerie at one of these camps, and she was clearly a gift from God to me, destined to be my wife and to stand by me in my calling.

Valerie was born into a church-going family but they were not born-again Christians. She heard about God but never understood the reality of being a sinner. After a tumultuous teenage period, Valerie met the Lord at the age of twenty through a physiotherapist and a friend who shared with her the truth of God and His love. The Lord regularly touched her heart through many circumstances, always it seemed to her just at the time she needed to know His love. Then her life complety changed when she got baptised and began to get involved in the local church where, after six years we met and got married.

According to the verse above, the Lord enabled myself and Valerie to do all that our hands could do in His service, including children's worship, children's radio, singing in the choir, worship leading, leading a house group and many other things. It was such a joy serving the Lord but we also discovered our weaknesses and a need to depend solely on Him.

Called into eldership

In 1992, when I was thirty-two years old, the Senior Pastor invited us to join the eldership of the Chandalier church, which at that time was located in the Avenue de Vizille in Grenoble. It was a bit of a shock because my understanding of eldership was that those involved needed to be at least fifty years old! I went to the Word of God to find a new understanding.

It is a trustworthy statement: if any man aspires to the office of overseer, it is a fine work he desires to do.

(1 Timothy 3:1)

Let no one look down on your youthfulness, but rather in speech, conduct, love, faith and purity, show yourself as an example of those who believe.

(1 Timothy 4:12)

We accepted this appointment and soon realised that there would be even more responsibilities than we had envisaged. This apostolic church consisted of about four hundred people, with about ten elders to assist the three pastors. The role of an elder is honourable but certainly not easy, often requiring the confronting of situations with no apparent human solutions. It was following one such delicate issue that Valerie and I became involved in setting up a family welcome team in the church. I can mention here that in our family we have three of our own children, Emilie, Emmanuel and Déborah, and also Rachel, who was welcomed and fostered in our family from 1995, encouraged by this scripture:

*Then He will answer them, "Truly I say to you, to the
extent that you did not do it to one of the least of these, you
did not do it to Me."*

(Matthew 25:45)

A burden for lost souls

As church elders we regularly took part in open-air
evangelistic events, which I must admit I really enjoyed.
Before my conversion, I had always been impressed that
these 'mad' Christians were willing to seemingly make fools
of themselves in public by singing and giving testimony
about their faith in Jesus. It appeared to me that they must
have really met with Jesus to have the strength to do such
crazy things. After my conversion, I realised that it was
only under the power of the Holy Spirit that they were able
to have such zeal to witness like that.

At this time, I learned three essential things with regard
to evangelism:

1. **There is a constant challenge to the church to
   wake up to God's call.**

   *For if I preach the gospel, I have nothing to boast of, for I
   am under compulsion; for woe is me if I do not preach the
   gospel.* (1 Corinthians 9:16)

2. **You cannot return from God-inspired evangelistic
   outreach without being filled with joy.**

   *The seventy return with joy, saying, "Lord, even the
   demons are subject to us in Your name."* (Luke 10:17)

3. **The devil does not like evangelism, but it is one of the best ways to gain victory over him. In any event he is just a deceiver**

   And they overcame him because of the blood of the Lamb and because of the word of their testimony, and they did not love their life even when faced with death. (Revelation 12:11)

CHAPTER 3

The vision of the Christian Fraternity and training in England

Calling into pastoral ministry

Over the years Valerie and I have been increasingly aware of the need for good discernment in regard to prophecy. When someone who is exercising the gift of prophecy is still needing inner healing themselves, they can be vulnerable to the enemy defiling that gifting. A true prophecy will encourage, edify and comfort and, when it includes direction, it will always confirm a deep conviction that has already been planted by the Holy Spirit into the spirit of the recipient.

Even while we were elders in the Chandelier church in Grenoble, we felt deep in our hearts that God was preparing us for something else, and a number of prophecies began to confirm these feelings. For example, one of the ladies in our house group shared with us a very clear prophetic vision:

she saw me dressed as a Roman soldier in full armour, with weapons ready for battle, waiting for precise orders.

At that time, we were looking for a bigger house for our growing family and we intended to buy a property to the south of Grenoble, near Vizille. This was the town where the plans for the French Revolution were birthed and it was a town where we had held evangelistic meetings on numerous occasions. One Thursday evening, the Senior Pastor called on me after a Bible study. He told me that there was a serious crisis within the leadership of one of the church plants, in a town called St Laurent du Pont. He wanted to invite me and Valerie to take on the role of pastoral care in this church, which was called the Christian Fraternity. He gave us three days to think it over, asking that we give him a reply on the following Sunday, so we had to make up our minds quickly.

Valerie and I decided to accept the invitation but it was truly an act of faith, encouraged by the prophetic vision that had been shared with us a few weeks earlier. These seemed to be the 'precise orders' that I had been waiting for. With hindsight, I do wonder, if we had been given more time to fully analyse the situation, whether we would have been so eager to respond to the Lord's calling! In the event, we found ourselves acting in accordance with the Bible, really living by faith.

But My righteous one shall live by faith; and if he shrinks
back, My soul has no pleasure in him.

(Hebrews 10:8)

We receive instructions

In appointing us to the new role, the Senior Pastor gave us the following advice:

1. I should keep my secular job.
2. We shouldn't move immediately, but commute to the church.
3. We should recognise that St Laurent-du-Pont church had a special calling.
4. We should be aware that the anointing on the church was very evident during summer seminars for visitors, but trouble seemed to return when normal church life resumed!

I find myself reflecting now on the lead up to this point in our lives. Valerie and I had worked with the Senior Pastor and his team for about thirteen years. Even though we had gone through one year of study at Dauphiné Bible Institute, the teaching we had received there was, in many ways, inadequate in preparing us to minister in a church, especially one that clearly had a particular calling.

We certainly saw very significant times of Holy Spirit anointing at the summer seminars each year, with people coming from all over France to hear powerful biblical teaching. However, although the seminars were not specifically intended to lead to deliverance ministry, there were, on occasions, difficult manifestations. We didn't know how to deal with these seemingly extreme aspects of deliverance which often caused Christians to be fearful of this kind of ministry.

Beginnings at St Laurent du Pont

We were sent to pastor the church at St Laurent du Pont in May 1998, with a very limited idea of the vision that God had given to the church. As we had been advised, I continued with my secular job so, during the first year of settling into the pastoral role, our family stayed every weekend in a house provided by the church. On the Saturday I made local pastoral visits and prepared for the Sunday service. On the Sunday afternoon we took the gospel to the elderly in hospital, or we visited those who had previously left the church. Then I planned the programme for the week ahead while Valerie looked after the children.

In the August of the same year, during a summer seminar, the Senior Pastor and his apostolic team laid hands on us both, formally releasing us into the leadership of the church at St Laurent du Pont.

While they were ministering to the Lord and fasting, the Holy Spirit said, "Set apart for Me Barnabas and Saul for the work to which I have called them." Then, when they had fasted and prayed and laid their hands on them, they sent them away.

(Acts 13:2-3)

Actually, we didn't fast on this occasion but there were a number of prophetic words spoken over us by the apostolic team. One of those words, in particular, needs to be recorded here. It prophetically foresaw the ministry of restoration that was later to be at the heart of our involvement with Ellel Ministries:

> *One day Jesus appeared before two disciples who were mending their nets. Patrick and Valerie, you are there, and you say in your heart, "I want to throw out the net." The Lord says, "Yes, but I am going to put into your hands new tools. There are nets you must repair and I, the Lord, will put into your hands these new tools, and I am going to teach you how to repair the nets. The Lord will bring to you many people whom you are going to train in how to repair nets."*

After a year of leading the church at St Laurent du Pont, the Lord gave us a house there, at a very reasonable price and without the need of a mortgage. The family soon settled into this new home, which was just right for our needs and, living in the town, I was able to undertake a more extensive pastoral ministry. The problem was that I was still working at Eybens, in a managerial role with the American multi-national company Hewlett Packard, commuting each day for between one and three hours, depending on traffic. Needless to say, I was having difficulty effectively balancing these different roles and I was heading for a breakdown, both emotionally and spiritually. However, by God's grace we were able to hold on.

Confirmation of vision

Some three years after we had taken up responsibility for the Christian Fraternity in St Laurent du Pont, some of the church members responsible for the Welcome House were discussing with us the service of inauguration for the church, which had taken place back in 1983. Unknown to me, at that meeting an elder had prophesied that the church was called, with regard to the local Body of Christ, to "wake up the sleeping sheaves", apparently a call to restore the people of God. I then remembered that this same elder had given me an almost identical prophecy at a cell-group meeting in 1986, at a time when I was totally unconnected with St Laurent du Pont.

As a result of this experience, I knew deep within me that this was the right place for Valerie and me. God had a more strategic plan than simply restoring spiritual order in the church and sorting out the relational difficulties, however important those might be. It was noticeable that, although these difficulties seemed to disappear with the new church leadership, they still remained simmering under the surface. I later understood the principle in the analogy of the persistence of many weeds: if the root is not dug up, no amount of cutting off at the surface will destroy it.

Useful preparation for the vision through my secular work

For twenty years, I had worked in different management positions with various companies, the last sixteen years with Hewlett Packard. I had learned, through a heavy workload, how to be flexible in the midst of change. In those twenty years I had had fifteen different management positions, looking after many different projects.

Hewlett Packard is a large international company, so I had opportunity for travel and for practising my English, particularly in European projects. The travelling was difficult to balance with my pastoral responsibilities, but the income from the company was important at that time and I didn't have a green light from the Lord to give up my professional work. Furthermore, it gave me very good experience in leading a team. With regard to the travelling, I actually remember feeling angry at having to take part in international meetings in English because of the extra effort it required in an already stressful environment! I remember crying out to God to give me the ability to understand the language, so that I could manage the work and also bring the Good News to the nations in due course.

However, learning the language was difficult for me. At school my teachers had considered me 'mediocre' in English, while better at German because it is more structured and phonetically easier for me to understand. So, to be honest, after a while I gave up trying to improve my English, as the technical environment in which I was immersed at

Hewlett Packard didn't provide sufficient opportunity for me to learn. In spite of this, something deep inside me was attracted to England and, in 1988, my wife and I spent our honeymoon in Rye, a little town on the South Coast of England. In fact, I had a number of opportunities to go to England, for both work and personal reasons.

God surely has a sense of humour. When the Senior Pastor introduced us to the church at St Laurent du Pont, he told them that I could play the guitar and I could speak English! The church members thought this very amusing as they could see no reason for the pastor to speak English in a little French town. What's more my level of English was still very poor. It was a good example of the gifting of an apostle. In this case the Senior Pastor was able to witness to things as they were to be, rather than as they were at that time.

> *Now faith is the assurance of things hoped for, the conviction of things not seen.*
>
> (Hebrews 11:1)

It's the moment for entering into full-time ministry

In 2002, returning from a conference in Mexico with the Senior Pastor and his wife, the Lord began to speak into my heart while I was sitting in the plane. It seemed that he was showing me that the time was approaching for me to leave my job. The Senior Pastor's wife told me their story of how God had called them to give up secular work and go into full-time ministry, and this powerfully witnessed to my spirit for my own situation.

In Hewlett Packard, just at that time, there were plans for a long-term reconstruction of the organisation, so I asked the Lord if this was the moment to leave secular employment. I recalled a prophecy, given twelve years before, that there would be an opening for me to serve the Lord full-time and I started thinking how best to deal with my resignation. My position in the company was not in any danger, with no risk of immediate redundancy. In fact, I was in quite an important position, needing to lay off workers in several of the company's French sites and I wondered if my resignation would be accepted.

Amazingly, when I approached my boss he was in favour, even giving encouragement to my plans for taking up a full-time role as a pastor. This felt like important confirmation that God was behind the whole idea. I felt that I had heard correctly so, with the approval of the church who had been praying, I left Hewlett Packard on 30 June 2003. What was even more amazing, the company proposed to take a measure of financial responsibility for the move to my new employment. This meant that I had the opportunity to look for a course which would help to train me in my new role as a pastor, and the company would pay for it up to a maximum of 3000 Euros. The offer had to be taken up before the end of September that year.

I started looking for a suitable Bible course and sent several emails to various Swiss organisations but had no replies. I looked at the possibility of a trip to Indonesia for an

apostolic conference, but realised that it didn't really have
what I wanted. Then one Sunday I was talking to François,
one of the young men from our church, about what I was
looking for and he told me about Ellel Ministries. He had
spent two years working as a volunteer at one of the Ellel
centres called Glyndley Manor, near Eastbourne in the
South of England. Francois was very enthusiastic about this
Ministry and encouraged me to look it up on the website.

Although I had never heard of Ellel Ministries, several
of the courses looked interesting, including a three-week
school at their centre in Australia. However, this started
in November, too late for the September deadline for the
financial assistance from the company. In fact, the only
course that fitted the right dates was at Glyndley Manor
and it was for nine weeks. This was a big problem because
I had no intention of leaving my wife and children for that
amount of time. I told Valerie about the course, expecting
her to also say, "No!" but her response was, "I'll pray about
it." Then, to my surprise, a few days later, she said that I
should attend this school.

I discussed it with the Senior Pastor, who was somewhat
reticent because of the effect on the church, but the elders
were in favour of my having this opportunity. For a while,
I felt pulled in various directions, concerned about what
would happen to the church, wondering if my English was
good enough, and worrying about how my children would
manage. In the end, I telephoned Glyndley Manor and
asked if they thought my English would be sufficient. The
co-ordinator of the Nine-Week School clearly had sufficient

faith in my language abilities, saying that he was quite sure that I would be able to follow the course effectively.

The other issue that concerned me was the intensity of the course and whether I would be able to get home during the nine weeks. I was reassured at being told there were three free weekends when I could visit my family. As I completed the application form, I was amazed to discover that the price of the school was 3015 Euros, almost exactly the limit of the financial offer from my employers for retraining, following my resignation. To be honest, without this funding, I would not have gone ahead with the school, as I really knew nothing about Ellel Ministries. But the Lord is good, and He knows us perfectly!

So I made preparations to leave for England on 20 September 2003, but some two weeks before that date, we heard of the death of the Senior Pastor. He had taken part in the church's summer seminars as usual but had been suffering from a long-term illness which had caused him a degree of suffering in the last few weeks. Because of all that we had shared together over the years, his death was a huge shock to us, as it was for many others. The last time I had spoken with him, we didn't speak about his health but rather about the course in England. As we talked, it seemed that the most important thing for him was what God had prepared for Valerie and me through this course I was going to attend. For him it was a vital link in the chain of God's purposes through us, and I reflected on how this apostle of Christ was carrying vision right up to the last minute of his life.

My time at Glyndley Manor

In the last few weeks before leaving for England, I felt the Lord's conviction that He was preparing something important for me through the course I was about to attend. When I arrived at the centre I was welcomed and shown to my room, which was to be shared with two other men, Kevin from England and Clive from South Africa. Both were already familiar with Ellel Ministries and had attended other courses. Like me, both had left behind a wife to spend nine weeks at Glyndley Manor, a time for receiving from the Lord.

In reality, I arrived at Glyndley Manor in a state of spiritual exhaustion, an accumulation of stress from my years of secular employment and now the responsibility of my new role as a pastor. Sometimes those around you don't recognise that you are near to burn-out, for this indeed was my situation. I'm so grateful to my wife who, during the time that I was waiting to go to England, always encouraged me to persevere in the call that God had placed on my life, to walk by faith into the future of full-time ministry.

So it was that, in this near-burn-out state, I began my first evening at Glyndley Manor. During the welcome meeting, I actually began to feel a little better, and during the praise time the presence of the Holy Spirit was so powerful that I found myself already receiving emotional healing without my having to do anything. I began to experience a dimension of love and spiritual security that I had never before known. In the previous five years there had been so many emotional traumas, including the death of our pastor, the death of two other brothers in Christ and the death of a missionary friend in Africa. I realised God was now bringing a precious time of personal restoration.

With my limitations in English, I found it difficult to understand all the finer points of the talks, but the Lord gave me the grace to receive ninety percent of the teaching. It was not so easy during the free times, mealtimes or when just relaxing with the other students. I realised that each culture has its own way of expressing thoughts and humourous comments, and I found it very difficult to communicate at a personal level. We were a group of forty-four students from twenty different nations, with nearly every continent represented. There were only two that were French-speaking, me and a Christian brother from the Congo.

From the very first week, I was powerfully aware of God's presence in the place. In particular, during the teaching entitled 'Walking under the Anointing of the Holy Spirit', I received a very special touch from God. Sometimes the gentleness of the teaching left me apprehensive, as it was so different from what I had known in the charismatic world that I was used to. The experience of two people listening to me and counselling me, sometimes for several hours, also touched me very deeply. As a pastor, I was familiar with being confronted by people with problems, but the willingness of the team to spend so much time with individuals was proof for me of the mark of God's love in this place.

Another thing challenged me: after some time at Glyndley Manor, I realised that, during my personal prayer and worship times, I no longer felt the need to spend so much time doing battle, through speaking in tongues, as the peace of the Lord surrounded me more and more each day. I later found out that the team at Glyndley Manor were interceding for each student, so we were all being covered in prayer.

During the teaching on the wounded heart, God very unexpectedly spoke to me about the spiritual state of France. Through Isaiah 61:1-2 He showed me the inner wounds of certain pastors and, in fact, of all the people of France. It was a very painful experience. I received a picture of refuse in a large dirty grey dustbin. I saw the lid of this dustbin very quickly opening and closing. What I saw inside was terrifying. It was a picture of the suffering experienced by some of God's servants in leadership, but also by many of God's children. It seemed to me that it was impossible to heal the depth of such suffering but, in that moment, I felt the Lord calling me to work in this special area.

Actually, in view of the depth of this wounding and suffering, I didn't really want to return to France to work in this area of ministry. I knew that this was the Lord's heart for the role of the shepherds of His people but I couldn't see how the Lord could accomplish such a task. I can only say now that it is indeed humanly impossible and it can only be done by the working of God's Spirit.

CHAPTER 4

My return to France and the work starts

New beginnings after the Nine-Week School

On my return to France I began full-time ministry. At the time of giving up my secular work I had been concerned about having too much time on my hands, and not knowing how to organise my life properly. I decided to structure each day as I had done during my professional life, going to the office at 8.30 am, having a break at midday and finishing about 6.00pm.

When I arrived home from the Nine-Week School, I had the pleasant surprise of finding my office completely transformed by a man from the church. He had received a vision from the Lord and had had the courage to carry out substantial alterations. I found myself in a completely refurbished office, with welcoming bright colours, space for my Bible and an English / French dictionary, a table and four

chairs for pastoral meetings and prayer ministry, exactly
what the Lord had prepared me for in my new direction
with Him.

Valerie recalls being particularly impacted by my
sharing with her the topic of healing from the effects of
accident and trauma. As I was explaining this, she felt as
if she was back again in the hospital ward where she had
stayed for fifty-four days after a car accident at the age of
eight. Eventually her physical body had been totaly healed
at the hospital but she hadn't realised the inner damage that
still remained from the trauma. As a result of a precious
time of her experiencing God's touch as I prayed for her,
she became very open to the ministry of inner healing and
was ready to join me in working towards establishing such
a ministry in France. God was clearly preparing her as well
as myself.

Setting up healing and deliverance seminars

Having been blessed through the teaching of Ellel
Ministries in England, I felt a responsibility for giving to the
local church more than just a simple report of what had
happened. I wanted to pass on to my brothers and sisters
in Christ the deep truths that I had learned. I cannot go
into detail in this book, but it seemed very necessary to me
that I should apply into the church in France what I had
been taught in England, particularly in areas the church
was fearful of pursuing. In fact, I considered these biblical
principles indispensable for training the disciples of Christ.

Go therefore and make disciples of all the nations,
baptizing them in the name of the Father and the Son
and the Holy Spirit, teaching them to observe all that I
commanded you; and lo, I am with you always, even to
the end of the age.

(Matthew 28:19)

The following topics describe the basis of what I now
regarded as essential teaching for the Body of Christ:

- **The important principle of God's spiritual covering over His children**

  He who dwells in) the shelter of the Most High will abide
  in the shadow of the Almighty. (Psalm 91:1-2)

- **The importance of our identity in Christ, and of our unconditional acceptance in belonging to God.**

  God created man in His own image, in the image of
  God He created him; male and female He created them.
  (Genesis 1:27)

- **The components of forgiveness and their significance in the healing of Christians.**

  And forgive us our debts, as we also have forgiven our
  debtors ... For if you forgive others for their transgressions,
  your heavenly Father will also forgive you. But if you do
  not forgive others, then your Father will not forgive your
  transgressions. (Matthew 6:12, 14-15)

- **The importance in relationships of the influence of soul-ties, both good and bad.**

  Do not be bound together with unbelievers; for what partnership have righteousness and lawlessness, or what fellowhip has light with darkness. (2 Corinthians 6:14)

- **The principle of generational blessings and curses, and the consequences of the sins of the fathers upon their children.**

  [You] who shows loving kindness to thousands, but repays the iniquity of fathers into the bosom of their children after them, O great and mighty God. The Lord of hosts is His name. (Jeremiah 32:18)

- **The principle of giving the devil no access in our life and the importance of this principle in the ministry of deliverance.**

  I will not speak much more with you, for the ruler of the world is coming, and he has nothing in Me.(John 14:30)

- **The principle that ground can be defiled by the sins of its inhabitants, and the influence that such ground can have back on its occupants.**

  Do not defile yourselves by any of these things; for by all these the nations which I am casting out before you have become defiled. For the land has become defiled, therefore I have brought its punishment upon it, so the land has spewed out its inhabitants. (Leviticus 18:24-25)

- **Healing of wounded hearts, healing for abused people and the effects of accident and trauma.**

  The Spirit of the Lord God is upon me, because the Lord has anointed me to bring good news to the afflicted; He has sent me to bind up the brokenhearted, to proclaim liberty to captives and freedom to prisoners. (Isaiah 61:1)

- **God's heart and plan for the sexuality of men and women.**

  For this reason a man shall leave his father and his mother, and be joined to his wife; and they shall become one flesh. (Genesis 2:24)

In December 2003, I decided to look up the notes that I had received on the Nine-Week School at Glyndley and translate them into French. I had two objectives in this: (1) to read them again and better understand certain areas which I had not absorbed during the school; and (2) to prepare a basic course of notes for teaching to the local church. I had permission from Ellel Ministries to do this provided that I was rewriting it in my own words and under my own name.

I wondered if I could put together a file of all these rewritten notes to distribute to the members of the church so that they could work on them and digest the teaching in their own time. I asked the Lord to show me if this was right with Him. Some days later a member of the church, who worked in a stationer's shop, came to ask me if the church needed any files! He had seven boxes of files that were no longer needed by his organisation and he wanted to give them to me. I took this as the Lord's reply!

I went ahead and organised the first two-day seminar for elders and leaders in the local church and for some people in other Christian organisations working among drug addicts. Twenty-nine people took part in that first seminar and they took away the files of notes. Comments about the weekend seminar were positive so I was encouraged to organise a second one for leaders and members of the Chandelier church in Grenoble, the central church of the group to which the church at St Laurent du Pont belonged.

While preparing for this second seminar, I asked a couple called John and Wendy Lewis to do some of the teaching. They were members of the Chandelier church and they had previously attended the same school in England as myself in 1996. In fact, they had been praying for the teaching of Ellel Ministries to be established in France and they had been the ones who had first encouraged François to go to Ellel at Glyndley Manor to join the Young People's Service Team. This was the young man from our church who had first given me the information about Ellel Ministries.

A helping hand from England

As I was praying about this second seminar, the Lord reminded me of a word He had given me at Glyndley Manor during one of the tea-breaks: "One day your room-mate Kevin Ford will be working with you." I was surprised by this as we were very different personalities and he didn't speak a word of French. At the school the three of us who shared a room, including Kevin, had prayed every night for our families and a real affection for one another had developed during that time. Kevin is happy for me to say here that he had had many struggles in his life over a period of at least eighteen years. During the school at Glyndley Manor, the Lord did a powerful work of healing and deliverance in his life. Kevin had also given me a written prayer, covering all the bondages associated with Freemasonry that he had experienced, and I had translated these pages for use in France.

So I telephoned Kevin in England and asked if he would be willing to come and give his testimony during the second seminar, particularly during the teaching on false religions and Freemasonry. To my surprise Kevin responded that he had just been asking the Lord for an opportunity for us to meet again and he was free to come. As a result, we set up the second seminar with my wife Valerie and myself, John and Wendy, Kevin, and a Mexican missionary couple, Luis and Graciela, who were working with us at the church. Without knowing it then, we were about to enter into an adventure far beyond our imagination! Within a short time, people were going to be deeply touched by the Word of God on the seminars, and we would be contacted by Christians from all over France looking for help.

Our church was already known for its summer conferences which it had been doing for some twenty-five years without a break. The participants had sometimes experienced a form of deliverance ministry that was carried out in a way accepted in French Christian circles at that time. In fact, the Senior Pastor was well known and had contacts in Switzerland, Belgium and in French-speaking African nations. It seemed that the vision for a ministry of restoration already had a good foundation. By February 2004 we had planned three more seminars, in April, August and October of that year. Kevin was able to help us with two of these, and to come for two weeks every month, at least for the first part of the year. From August onwards he was committed to a new job in London.

During the months we spent working together and praying with people, I completed the translation and revision of my teaching notes and we experienced God's amazing touch on people's lives day after day. Kevin had particular discernment for the needs of inner healing, while the Lord gave me a powerful authority in areas of deliverance. It seemed that God had arranged His pairing of the two of us for pioneering this new healing ministry in France. When Kevin returned to England we continued with the seminars because of the demand that was coming from God's people. By the end of 2004 one hundred and thirty people had received teaching on the seminars and over one hundred people had received personal healing prayer ministry.

We became increasingly aware of the importance of this ministry when we saw the price that some people were willing to pay to come to these seminars from the four corners of France. They came from La Rochelle, Mulhouse and even Ajaccio on Corsica, sometimes travelling for a whole day, each way, just to attend a two-day seminar.

Establishing the seminars and preparing for a school of deliverance

Looking at the needs of both the local church and also the wider Body of Christ in France, we arranged a series of three seminars: an introduction to the healing ministry, one on deliverance and inner healing, and one dealing with marriage and sexuality. As the work developed, I became increasingly aware of the need to train disciples of Jesus. In fact, I have always had this principle on my heart: the necessity for teamwork both in evangelism and pastoral care. I believe that growth in the Body of Christ can only happen by training disciples and forming teams for carrying out God's Kingdom work.

> *Go therefore and make disciples of all the nations, baptizing them in the name of the Father and the Son and the Holy Spirit, teaching them to observe all that I commanded you; and lo, I am with you always, even to the end of the age.*
>
> (Matthew 28:19-20)

In September 2004, we had a retreat for all the pastors belonging to the churches associated with the Christian Fraternity in St Laurent du Pont. We prayed for each other and for the particular congregations for which we were each responsible. I shared the vision that I had for St Laurent du

Pont, to organise a school of deliverance and inner healing. I deliberately timed this school for the summer, a season when it would not be seen as unusual, as our church was known for its summer gatherings. It seemed to me that by offering a three-week school, the participants could really get to grips with the teaching. The programme was worked out on the basis of John Lewis and me teaching the principles of deliverance and inner healing, with pastors from the other churches teaching the more familiar topics that were already covered in the Bible college at Grenoble.

Planning carefully, to recognise the sensitivity of the topics

Having worked in management for twenty years, I understood the vital importance of carefully forming a leadership team. Biblical deliverance is little understood in France, and indeed it is the same in many other countries, so the teaching on this topic inevitably causes a degree of opposition. It was just the same at the time of Jesus. He and His disciples were often confronted by the religious leaders.

As they were going out, a mute, demon-possessed man was brought to Him. After the demon was cast out, the mute man spoke; and the crowds were amazed, and were saying, "Nothing like this has ever been seen in Israel." But the Pharisees were saying, "He casts out demons by the ruler of the demons."

(Matthew 9: 32-34)

The deliverance ministry was sometimes not well received even by the people Jesus was trying to help.

> *Those who had seen it [the deliverance by Jesus of the Gerasene demoniac] described to them how it had happened to the demon-possessed man, and all about the swine. And they began to implore Him to leave their region.*
>
> (Mark 5: 16-17)

I had learned from both my Christian training and the experience of secular employment the importance of respecting rightful authority, an issue sadly lacking in much of the church. If we want God's people to be blessed and live in the freedom they need, it is absolutely essential for the local church to be touched by the truth of the Kingdom of God. That truth needs to be communicated on behalf of the Lord to all His children, within a safe structure of rightful authority.

> *Every person is to be in subjection to the governing authorities. For there is no authority except from God, and those which exist are established by God.*
>
> (Romans 13:1)

> *You younger men, likewise, be subject to your elders; and all of you, clothe yourself with humililty toward one another, for God is opposed to the proud, but gives grace to the humble.*
>
> (1 Peter 5:5)

I then shared with the pastoral team at St Laurent du Pont the possibility of organising a course for all the leadership within our group of churches, to be led by a visiting Ellel Ministries team. Since I needed to prepare for this, in April 2004 I went to Glyndley Manor for a pastor's healing weekend with Christian Rivière, the chairman of the group of churches. It was here that we made contact with the Centre Directors David and Denise Cross. Christian and I arranged with them to come for a one week seminar for all the leading pastoral team from the Grenoble group of churches. The idea was favourably received back home and twenty-six pastors and their wives booked in for this course in February 2005.

Praise God that it was a success. David and Denise, together with another couple from Glyndley Manor, Roy and Rosalind, came to teach for five days at a time when the church property was covered in snow! A number of the leaders and their wives were touched by the teaching. I was personally set free and healed from an issue of control, and my wife was healed from the effects of a trauma she had experienced through an accident when she was eight years old.

God sends reinforcements into His camp

While preparing for this course, I was asking God for confirmation of the vision of future healing seminars and for help in making them effective. One evening during the autumn of 2004 I unexpectedly received a word from the

Lord via a text message from Kevin Ford, who had been working in London. This is what he said, "The vision that you have for the Christian Fraternity, and for the freedom of God's people in France, comes from God. What is more, He is asking me to join you and help you in this mission. I have seen my pastor and he is ready to provide some financial support to my wife and I. I have already told my boss that I am leaving so, as from January, I shall be available to work with you in France."

At the time of Kevin's message, I was in fact receiving some opposition from the local church, probably over concerns about the ministry of deliverance. So this offer of assistance came as a precious confirmation from God, a strengthening and a great encouragement for me to persevere with the vision. Because our church had no means of fully financing Kevin and his wife Daniela, I felt it right to ask Kevin if he could arrange for us all to meet with his pastor. Valerie and I had actually already planned a visit to England at the beginning of 2005 and so we were able to meet the pastor of the large Anglican church where Kevin was a member. After just a half an hour of being together, the pastor decided that the missions department of the church could contribute £1000 to help in pioneering the new work in France, as well as providing further finance, pending approval from the church council, to support Kevin and Daniela personally. What an encouragement!

Kevin had already resigned from his job by then so, when we returned to France, he started to minister with me while Daniela continued to work in London. This was a necessary temporary measure while waiting for the church council to give the green light for the regular support of the couple. During this time, Kevin and I spent many hours talking to, and praying with, Christians in the local church, and with many others who had assisted at the previous seminars and were crying out for the ministry of healing to be continued.

Sometimes we had four or five ministry sessions in a day and the Lord was moving us forward in understanding the enemy's strategies and the powerful principles of healing in the Kingdom of God. Deliverance, which had previously taken many hours, was being completed in minutes as we recognised and closed the doors which had been used by the powers of darkness. The enemy is a legalist, knows the Word of God and knows his rights, but these are removed by confession of sins, forgiving those who have caused offence, and sometimes dealing with the spiritual inheritance. We learnt each day that, when biblical principles and the ordinances of God are put into practice in our lives, the freedom that God wants for His children can be appropriated without there needing to be a long spiritual struggle.

My people are destroyed for lack of knowledge

(Hosea 4:6a)

Often we found that, by asking the Lord to cut all ungodly soul-ties in wrong relationships, once the person had both confessed any sin and forgiven those involved, effective results followed in the ministry of deliverance. One of the areas of understanding into which the Lord led us was the issue of generational iniquity and its effect on people's lives, especially where some family members had been involved with activities such as Freemasonry and the occult.

We understood that the devil can use the sins of forbears and a parent's lack of spiritual covering to infiltrate the lives of children in the family. One example of this was with a teenage girl who came with her Christian parents. She had been having horrible nightmares of being raped despite never having had any sexual relations. When the girl and her parents forgave the grandparents for their sexual sin, to everyone's amazement, she was delivered in a very short time.

Another example was of a young woman who had had a car accident while driving along a dangerous section of road near Toulon. She had been travelling with three young men who were under the influence of alcohol. Following the accident this young woman had herself developed a problem with alcohol and was unable to progress in her spiritual life.

As we ministered to her, the Lord reminded her that her grandfather had been an alcoholic. The Lord showed us that this had made her vulnerable to a spiritual inheritance in the area of alcoholism. She forgave her grandfather and the young men in the car. We also realised that this stretch of road was spiritually defiled through previous accidents, and that this had added to the opportunity for the enemy to take advantage of her at that time. As we asked the Lord to release her from the effects of her grandfather's sin, to release her from the ungodly ties with the young men, and to set her free from the spiritual influence over that part of the Toulon road, she was clearly delivered and completely set free from her alcoholism.

Learning while ministering

The Holy Spirit particularly led us to apply four biblical principles:

1. Confession of sin

If we confess our sins, He is faithful and righteous to forgive us our sins and to cleanse us from all unrighteousness. (1 John 1:9)

2. Forgiving those who have offended us

For if you forgive others for their transgressions, your heavenly Father will also forgive you. But if you do not forgive others, then your Father will not forgive your transgressions. (Matthew 6:14-15)

3. Confessing (agreeing with God about) the sins of our forbears

Our fathers sinned, and are no more; it is we who have born their iniquities. (Lamentations 5:7)

So those of you who may be left will rot away because of their iniquity in the lands of your enemies; and also because of the iniquities of their forefathers they will rot away with them. If they confess their iniquity and the iniquity of their forefathers, in their unfaithfulness which they committed against Me, and also in their acting with hostility against Me... then I will remember My covenant... I will remember the land. (Leviticus 26:39-40, 42a)

4. Seeking freedom from the spiritual influence of a locality which has been polluted by the sins of inhabitants.

Do not defile yourselves by any of these things; for by all these the nations which I am casting out before you have become defiled. For the land has become defiled, therefore I have brought its punishment [iniquity] upon it, so the land has spewed out its inhabitants. (Leviticus 18:24-25)

We understood that each principle had specific importance. The Lord showed us how to close each door by which the enemy had obtained access into the life of the person who had come to us for help. Sadly, I do not have space in this book to record all the experiences that we had during this time. But I know that when we apply the biblical principles, such as those I have mentioned, we truly see the manifestation of the Kingdom of God and the transformation of precious lives.

Visits to other churches

During one of our seminars, we had a church leader from Avignon. Initially he came for prayer, but then he was looking for training in order to establish a pastoral and healing team in his own church. It seemed to me that this church had a clear and sound vision for a healing ministry. They understood the importance of a ministry team coming alongside the pastor to support him, and preparing the church to welcome new converts, similar to the way Jesus trained the first disciples.

The church in Avignon invited us in 2004 and 2005 to train their leaders, and we saw the fruitfulness of the teaching from Ellel and how important it was even amongst the leaders. One example was in the teaching about the effects of Freemasonry. As we went through the prayers on this topic, we experienced a powerful encounter with the Spirit of God bringing clear freedom to almost half of the leadership team.

Since that time I have had the opportunity to visit a number of churches in Paris, Toulouse and Montpellier, for example. I can honestly say that at each of these places there has been significant blessing from the teaching that God has given through Ellel Ministries.

The need for more courses

Working with Kevin, John and Wendy, and a team from our local church, I soon became aware of the importance of the experience Ellel Ministries had gained by practising over the previous twenty years, ministering deliverance and restoration into broken lives. I had not been able to find an equilvalent ministry in France, and I say this in all humility, knowing and respecting the deliverance ministries that do exist in the country. I have personally been aware of and practised deliverance since 1986 but, within Ellel Ministries, I have seen a particular maturity in this area not apparent elsewhere.

I am persuaded that the ministry of healing and deliverance is indispensable for the growth of the church in France. However, I have understood that it must be exercised in a biblical manner, in a safe spiritual environment, with experienced people anchored into the Word of God, and people rightly submitted to the covering of an appropriate authority structure. Another strength of the teaching of Ellel is that the ministry of inner healing is not separated from the ministry of deliverance, in line with how Jesus sent out the first disciples, and how He instructed them to teach new disciples.

> *And Jesus came up and spoke to them, saying, "All authority has been given to Me in heaven and on earth. Go therefore and make disciples of all the nations, baptizing them in the name of the Father and the Son and the Holy Spirit, teaching them to observe all that I commanded you; and lo, I am with you always, even to the end of the age."*
>
> (Matthew 28:18-20)

One illustration is sometimes more effective than lengthy explanations. Imagine a shepherd out on the hills taking care of his sheep. His role is to lead the flock to good pasture where they can feed themselves. This has been the role of disciples leading believers to good spiritual food, but what happens if a sheep gets caught in a barbed-wire fence? How can this sheep get to the good food while gripped by the barbed-wire? Clearly it needs first to be set free from the place where it is held captive. This is the ministry of deliverance.

Now imagine this wounded sheep set free but without attention to the wounds from the barbed-wire. It's very likely that the condition of the sheep will worsen through the wounds becoming infected. Disinfectant and healing are needed before it can begin to feed itself on the good pasture. For believers, the disinfectant comes in the form of repentance and forgiveness so that inner healing can take place, an essential process, even if it takes some time.

From my own observation, deliverance represents about 15% of the restoration process while inner healing and walking daily in the life of a disciple are perhaps 85%. Although the lesser part of the process, the deliverance is absolutely essential for the person to walk on in freedom.

At this point in our journey of discovering a new dimension to the deliverance ministry, we realised that there were times when we failed to understand what was happening and we needed more guidance. I will give an example of this.

One day we were ministering to a 40-year-old lady I will call Alice. She had had a very damaging childhood, loosing her mother at the age of eight and her father had remarried several times in his desperation to deal with his loss. During the ministry there had been powerful deliverance related to generational iniquity from ancestors involved in Freemasonry and Nazism. There had also been difficult issues of forgiveness for Alice to work through, particularly involving her grandmothers. It became clear, as the Holy Spirit led both Alice and ourselves, that she had been abused around the age of two or three. To our surprise as we talked, Alice began to go on all fours and speak like a three-year-old child.

As we gently spoke to her, Alice started telling us in a child's voice all that had happened to her, about abuse that had been witnessed, she said, only by her teddybear. The Holy Spirit led us to adapt our conversation with her to language appropriate for a three-year-old and we tried to speak carefully to her about Jesus. But it was clear that this child-part of Alice didn't know Him and, in fact, that 'little Alice' was full of rebellion against Jesus, despite 'adult Alice' walking with the Lord today. With the help of the Holy Spirit we were able to persevere patiently with bringing this trapped part of Alice into God's freedom and healing, so that the Lord could continue with His restoring work in her life.

As I have previously mentioned, I have been deeply moved by the Holy Spirit since hearing the teaching on the wounded heart and the need for healing of the human spirit. During the Nine-Week School in England, there were three sessions on fragmentation of the human spirit and soul. While listening to the topic, I found myself crying deeply, under the anointing of the Holy Spirit, but my mind was unable, at that time, to fully take in these teachings.

Just at this time, I received an invitation from Peter Horrobin to go to England and take part in an advanced course, dealing particularly with the issue of inner fragmentation. This was a course, which took place every two years, especially for those who had already completed one of the foundational Ellel Ministries schools. I felt in my heart that this was indeed the right time to take this advanced course at Ellel Grange, near Lancaster, the centre that is the hub of the international work of the Ministry. This was at the end of the summer of 2005.

More miraculous provision

Because of the importance of this 15-day course, I decided this time that I would participate with my wife Valerie. She had not attended a long course like this before, even though she had been on almost all the seminars that had already been organised in France. We were able to receive some sponsorship from Ellel Grange, but I felt that God also wanted Kevin to attend the course. He had been working with us in France for most of the previous eighteen months, for three weeks at a time, and I believed that we should be covering the cost of the course for Kevin.

For the Scripture says, "You shall not muzzle the ox while he is threshing," and "The laborer is worthy of his wages."
(1 Timothy 5:18)

The total cost for the three of us was to be about 4000 Euros. It so happened that this was just the amount that I had managed to save from the settlement of my departure from my employer two years previously. However, I had had in my heart the need to put this money aside for my children's education, while at the same time I didn't want to rely on the local church to provide the funds.

That same week when I was with my son at a Grenoble business centre, I met a colleague from the organisation, Hewlett Packard, that I had previously worked for. He had left at the same time as myself. As we talked, I realised that I had taken the step of faith in leaving the company just at the right time, two years earlier. It became apparent that I would not have been eligible for the current financial package, which had now been restricted to other categories of employees.

What was even more amazing was that I discovered from this colleague that, as an employee of the company, I had automatically received some company shares many years before which were apparently lodged in an account in a bank in Paris. I managed to contact the bank and, on receiving my employee number, they were able to advise me that I owned shares in the company to the value of 4000 Euros, which was exactly what was needed to cover the cost of the three of us for the course.

I realised again that God is no man's debtor. He wanted to supply both my needs and that of the local church, and He wanted to show me that He, and He alone, was going to be in charge of this project right from its birth. Alleluia!

More confirmation of God's hand

As I have explained, at the time that I was called with my wife to pastor the church in St Laurent du Pont I also had a responsible position with Hewlett Packard, and I was promised further responsibility in the future. For a long time I had wanted more opportunities to serve the Lord, so being given more responsibility in the company was in conflict with my vision for ministry.

Yet somehow, over a period of five years, God helped me to balance both the secular and pastoral roles, even as my responsibilities grew within the company. Then one day my director came to see me and asked if I would represent Hewlett Packard (France) on several European and global projects. It all seemed too much, with the rest of my heavy workload at three different sites in France, but somehow I felt it right to accept the instruction.

> *Submit yourselves for the Lord's sake to every human institution...*
>
> (1 Peter 2:13)

The key issue was that I really needed to improve my English to take on the task. I cried out to the Lord to make sense of this demanding requirement, by asking that one day I would need this language to preach the Kingdom of God in nations other than France.

I can say today that God took me at my word and that I have had to preach and give testimony many times in English since that time, in countries such as Bulgaria, Ukraine, England, USA and Switzerland. While on the advanced course in Lancaster, the Ellel representatives from both Germany and Holland came to see me to discuss working together in the development of Ellel Ministries in Europe. It was in that moment that the Holy Spirit spoke to me, "Now you understand why I asked you to manage the European projects in Hewlett Packard. It was to prepare you."

Samuel said, "Has the Lord as much delight in burnt offerings and sacrifices as in obeying the voice of the Lord?

(1 Samuel 15:22a)

CHAPTER 5

Partnership between Ellel Ministries and the Christian Fraternity

Invitation to Peter Horrobin and preparation for the first Two-Week School for Ellel Ministries in France

Following the visit by David and Denise Cross in February 2005 for a course with pastors and their wives from the evangelical churches in the local area, the enthusiasm was unanimous. As a result, we considered the possibility of an invitation to Peter Horrobin, the International Director of Ellel Ministries, to come and speak at the next annual conference of ministers from around France, held at Grenoble.

This conference was always organised by a committee made up of representatives from many churches, including some from the Grenoble team. After a number of discussions, it was decided to invite Peter Horrobin to be one of the speakers at the 2006 conference, a gathering which represented the Charismatic Movement in France. It had been held over several decades each year in March and was attended by 400-500 pastors and leaders. The purpose was to come together and share experiences in the evangelical trends within the country.

From the time of the pastors conference at St Laurent du Pont in 2005, I had been discussing with David Cross, who was the Ellel Ministries Regional Director for Western Europe, my vision for setting up a healing and deliverance school. At the time we were just a small team and I had drawn up a draft programme of courses for a two-week school in the summer. David proposed that Ellel Ministries could assist with this, but I needed to have the agreement of the Senior Pastor, Christian Rivière, who provided the spiritual covering for my ministry. He was the president of the group of churches to which our church at St. Laurent du Pont belonged.

We decided to go together to Ellel Grange in June 2005 for Christian to become more acquainted with Ellel Ministries and to begin to plan both the ministers' conference in Grenoble (including the invitation to Peter Horrrobin) and the framework for collaboration with Ellel on the proposed school of healing and deliverance at St. Laurent du Pont.

We had two alternatives for organising this school:

1. The Christian Fraternity would invite an Ellel Ministries team to come and share teaching during the

three-week series of seminars on the theme of healing
and deliverance. For more than 25 years the church
at St Laurent du Pont had become used to hosting
seminars involving visiting international speakers, so
we felt comfortable that this option was manageable
for us. It would mean that the Ellel Ministries speakers
and teaching would be under the spiritual covering
of the Christian Fraternity, in the same way as had
happened each year with other speakers.

2. The other option was to have a school fully
   organised and under the responsibility and spiritual
   covering of Ellel Ministries. This arrangement would
   be very different from our normal way of hosting
   summer seminars, but the right spiritual covering for
   this significant area of teaching was something I just
   knew we had to get right.

Having participated previously in Ellel Ministries events
such as a series of seminars over three days at Glyndley
Manor, I recognised the disciplined way in which the
teaching was given. I felt the Lord say that this was the
way He wanted the teaching to be done in our church,
and eventually throughout France. God had shown me the
enormous need for the healing and deliverance ministry
in the nation, and He made it clear that He wanted it to
be provided in His way. I realised that the vision God had
given me could most easily and quickly be carried out by
Ellel Ministries becoming established in France, taking

full advantage of the experience Ellel had gained since its inception in 1986. Incidentally, it was very significant for me that 1986 was the same year that I had personally received my most powerful experiences of deliverance.

I also knew that in this area of ministry, particularly that involving deliverance, it was important not to be working alone. My twenty years of experience with just a small team of prayer ministers had actually put me off this area of ministry, because of the challenges of needing the right spiritual covering. So, with all this in mind, and with the agreement of Christian Rivière, the second option was chosen.

I realised that letting Ellel Ministries take the lead in establishing the seminars in France, meant giving up something of my personal reputation. However, I knew that, although Peter Horrobin was the founder and primary vision-carrier of the work of Ellel, the organisation was not simply built around him. It was structured through teamwork, all the members rightly submitted to one another, working in more than twenty centres around the world and always seeking to be led by the Holy Spirit.

The importance of Godly structure and spiritual covering

It is so important that a ministry such as Ellel should be led by spiritually competent people, working under an established spiritual covering. I had experienced good covering in the local church organisation and I was reassured to see this throughout Ellel Ministries. Through many years of ministry, Ellel had developed a safe structure for teaching, healing and deliverance. To be honest, this type of structure is not very easily put in place within the culture of the Body of Christ in France. Even from a secular viewpoint, having worked for many years in an American multinational company, I knew the strength and efficiency that results from a good structure and disciplined work practice.

It's interesting to look at the story of Moses in the book of Exodus. Moses had received a call to lead the people out of Egypt, and God's favour was on him. His father-in-law Jethro saw that the hand of God was on Moses and rejoiced in all that God had done for the Children of Israel through his leadership.

Jethro rejoiced over all the goodness which the Lord had done to Israel, in delivering them from the hand of the Egyptians.

(Exodus 18:9)

However, one day when Moses was passing judgement on a dispute concerning the people, Jethro saw all that he was having to do and told Moses that going it alone like that would eventually just wear him out.

Moses' father-in-law said to him, "The thing that you are doing is not good. You will surely wear out, both yourself and these people who are with you, for the task is too heavy for you; you cannot do it alone."

(Exodus 18:17-18)

The advice from Jethro was to structure the work by organising a capable team to cover the work, using men of integrity who feared God and who were not after their own gain. This way the workload could be effectively shared.

"Furthermore, you shall select out of all the people able men who fear God, men of truth, those who hate dishonest gain; and you shall these over them as leaders of thousands, of hundreds, of fifties and tens. Let them judge the people at all times; and let it be that every major dispute they will bring to you, but every minor dispute they themselves will judge. So it will be easier for you, and they will bear the burden with you. If you do this thing and God so commands you, then you will be able to endure, and all these people also will go to their place in peace."

(Exodus 18:21-23)

This principle of rightful delegation is essential in establishing vision, and this is what I had witnessed in Ellel Ministries. I can say today that, throughout its international work, I have witnessed an efficient building of the vision that God had given. All the teaching is validated by the Ellel International Executive, a group made up from the centres around the world, and in the Executive meetings experiences are shared, discussed, put to prayer and recorded. This has kept a clear history and accountability for the development of the work.

The foundational vision for Ellel (to welcome, teach and heal, as in Luke 9:11), together with the practices of the Ministry, are carefully passed on to every new centre which the Lord has raised up throughout the world. This is is accordance with scripture.

> *The things which you have heard from me in the presence of many witnesses, entrust these to faithful men who will be able to teach others also.*

(2 Timothy 2:2)

It has also been important within the Ministry to seek out faithful men and women, chosen by God, to teach and minister to others within the organisation. It has been equally important for there to be a spiritual heritage, for future generations, through books written on the teaching that God has entrusted to the Ministry. All of these ways of working are also found in many other Ministries but I have recognised afresh that this is a vital strategy if the work is to be longlasting.

The first Ellel France Summer School, Healing Retreats and a Modular School

Once the strategic decision had been taken to establish Ellel Ministries in France, we began to put the vision into place, despite only having a small team of people – Michèle, a part-time secretary, John and Wendy Lewis, my wife and me. The thirteen-day Summer School included forty-two teaching sessions which had to be translated, printed and collated. There was also information about Ellel Ministries, ministry procedures and copyright notices to produce. All this documentation needed to be in both English and French as we were expecting students from five different nations and some did not speak French.

After this first Summer School in 2006, we managed to produce similar material for a Modular School (series A and B), to be taught on one weekend every month over two years. In 2007 we also began holding Healing Retreats, to a pattern being used in every Ellel centre: two trained ministry team members praying for two people alternately over two days, the prayer times being punctuated by six teaching sessions of about 25 minutes each.

The Modular School, Healing Retreats and the Summer School all continued over the subsequent years, together with seminars on specific topics developed by the Ellel Team in France, such as *Catholicism in the light of the Bible*. In February 2009 we had the first Ellel Ministries International Conference in France, in collaboration with the Chandelier group of churches. Peter and Fiona Horrobin came to teach, along with other team members from the UK. About 250 people attended and this was a great encouragement to the Ellel France team. Ellel Ministries in France was truly becoming established.

CHAPTER 6

Establishing a healing centre

The importance of a place to welcome people

In the vision that Peter Horrobin, founder of Ellel Ministries received in 1976, the text of Luke 9:11 became one of the foundations of the work:

> *But he crowds were aware of this and followed Him; and welcoming them, He began speaking to them about the Kingdom of God and curing those who had need of healing.*
>
> (Luke 9:11)

In 1986 the first healing center for the Ministry was birthed at Ellel Grange near Lancaster. It is clearly in the heart of Jesus to welcome the needy and, for this to be possible, it's sometimes necessary to have a place dedicated to that welcome, a place where people can stay for a while away from their daily routines and concerns.

As I explained in chapter two, at the start of my Christian life I experienced several deliverances which were a springboard for my spiritual life. I remember one deliverance in particular that I would like to give as an example, to illustrate the importance of having a place set apart for exercising the important ministry of restoration in people's lives.

When I was teenager, around the age of 18, I went on a caving trip with my cousin and uncle, along with some of their friends who were experienced cavers. We were going to explore a cave in the Vercors, but we first had to cross a small underground lake with a small inflatable boat, then climb a vertical wall of about eight meters before we could actually enter the cave. When we climbed the rock face, I slipped because my shoes were not really suitable for climbing. I remember that, despite having been tied with a rope, experiencing one of the most frightening moments of my life, causing shivers throughout my body.

Later, after I became a Christian, I was one day being prayed for by a leader of the church to which I belonged. We were in the hallway of the church when another pastor, who was passing by and saw that they were praying for me, had a picture of a black hole. He asked if I had ever been caving. At that precise moment to my astonishment I screamed out, "Don't touch me, don't touch me!" In fact, it wasn't me screaming, but a demon that had just been unmasked, and which had clearly entered me in the moment of fear in the cave. I was delivered and set free there in the church hallway. Hallelujah!

The problem was that several people who were in this hallway heard me scream and this made me somewhat embarrassed. I am not one for formalities but I think you will agree with me that the whole incident would have been more comfortable for me, and less humiliating, if this release had happened in a safe place, away from others who might be affected.

The vision of the Christian Fraternity

The Senior Pastor, who had an apostolic ministry, also carried in his heart a vision for the ministry of deliverance. He was acutely aware of the state of the Church and its need for restoration. In his desire for the advancement of Kingdom of God, he was looking for a place where people could come to be welcomed and restored. When, in 1979, he visited the site that we today call the Christian Fraternity, in St Laurent du Pont, God clearly spoke to him, telling him that this was the place He had chosen for helping people with spiritual needs.

Since 1981 this site has been used mightily by God to bless and encourage His people, by hosting teaching seminars. It was managed for seventeen years by Pastor Michel Dal Pont (who incidentally is now an associate teacher with Ellel Ministries) and since 1998 by me. From that time, as you have heard, God has enabled us to continue the work under the covering of Ellel Ministries. I believe that this has provided us with quality teaching and tools, which have made it possible for us to take a leap forward of some fifteen

years in implementing the restoration ministry, particularly
in the area of inner healing.

The need to increase reception capacity

As soon as Ellel Ministries arrived in 2006 I began to
understand that the current reception and accommodation
capacity would be insufficient if using only the house bought
by the church in 1979. We had the capacity in the church
building to hold nearly 400 people for teaching sessions but,
in the building used for accommodation, we were limited
to just fifteen people in guest rooms.

Just as we were preparing for the first Ellel summer
school, in 2006, our neighbour came knocking on the door
asking if we were interested in buying his house which was
immediately adjoining the church property. We carefully
examined the offer for the house which had a floor area
of 350 m^2 and grounds of 2500 m^2, at an overall price of
600,000 Euros.

The offer was shared with the delegates on the summer
school and this resulted in amazing donations amounting
to 37,000 Euros, but we needed to consider prayerfully
whether this purchase was God's will for us at that time.
The seller had previously lowered the price, but we felt
that it was still too high. Actually, I had in my heart a much
smaller amount for this house although, of course, it was a
sum we still didn't have.

There were several potential buyers for the house,
including a developer who was prepared to make a

substantial offer to allow a construction project on the land which would have overlooked the church property. This would have been very detrimental to the setting of the church, but we had neither the money nor the conviction to outbid the developer in order to obtain this property. The project to establish an Ellel welcome-centre was therefore placed back into the hands of God and, to our great surprise, the owner agreed to sell to someone else at a price lower than the price offered by the developer. So the construction project did not take place and we were confident that the Lord had not given a green light for the purchase of this particular house. With the permission of the donors, the 37,000 Euros were put into a fund to be used for promoting a partnership between Ellel Ministries and the church, a ten-year agreement which was duly signed by both parties.

Buying a new house: 'Le Refuge'

Always having in mind the insufficient accommodation capacity for the work of Ellel Ministries at the church, I regularly scrutinised the properties for sale in the estate agents in St Laurent du Pont. One day when I was looking at the offers in one of the agencies, I noticed a three-story house with twelve rooms for sale at a price of 160,000 Euros. What caught my attention was the price. Although it seemed that a lot of work would need to be done on the house, the price was still very good and certainly much more affordable than the house we were previously offered in 2006.

With the potential of 300 m² in floor area, this offer was very interesting, but I didn't immediately sense the Lord telling me to approach the estate agent. Then a few days later, as I was walking down the street next to the church, to my surprise, I saw the house which was in the estate agent's window and it was almost opposite our guest house on the church property. I hadn't realised before, from the information at the estate agent, that this was the house for sale.

Encouraged by this, and feeling that the Lord was prompting me, I decided to knock on the door of the house. An elderly lady opened it and I just asked her the question directly: "Is your house for sale?" She was very surprised but told me that yes it was, and she wondered how I knew about it. I didn't tell her that the Lord had led my steps, but asked if I could come in and look at the property.

She let me explore the first and second floors and the attic, and I immediately saw the potential of the house, but it still seemed crazy because we didn't have the money. When I went back downstairs the owner showed me the documents relating to the estate agent and, since there was no exclusivity clause with this agency, the sale could legitimately be done directly between the buyer and seller, which would save us 9000 Euros. I explained to her about the project to make guest rooms for increasing the welcoming capacity of the Fraternity, and it became clear that the lady was already convinced that we were going to buy her property.

I remember telling her that it would be necessary first to

have the approval of the mayor before we could procede with providing a guest house, and inside I was thinking, "But we don't have the money, so don't get carried away." But right at that moment I heard the Lord say to me, "Talk about it to Lucette." I would like to make it clear here that I don't hear God talking to me in that way every day! However, I just knew that God was challenging me in that particular situation and I had to talk to Lucette about it. She was a member of the church but was often travelling abroad and she was actually away at that particular time. When she returned I explained what had happened about the house and how I was supposed to speak to her.

She immediately gave a shudder and told me that the Lord had spoken to her during the trip abroad, saying that she was to prepare herself for a project. She told me straightway that she would be willing to donate something towards the purchase of the house and, after praying about it, she came back to me and told me that a recent investment would make it possible to finance more than 50% of the cost of the project, and she wanted to do this in obedience to God. From that moment I knew that what had initially been just a dream was now becoming a reality.

Signs from the Lord about purchasing 'The Refuge'

As I have mentioned, before we could proceed with any purchase, it was necessary to consult the local planning department at the town hall to see if we would be permitted to have this project of a guest house accepted. One difficulty with the house was that it only had one very steep staircase, and that could be a problem for evacuation of the public in the event emergency.

So I made an appointment with the mayor of St Laurent du Pont to discuss the project and also to have a general discussion with him about the relationship between the church the town authorities. After discussing the points concerning the church, I told him about the purchase plan for the house. To my surprise, he was already aware of the sale and he was particularly concerned about a developer who wanted to buy the property in order to build four apartments. When I explained our project, to create a private guest house with five rooms to accommodate a maximum of fifteen people, all in accordance with planning regulations, he was very receptive and very positive about the whole scheme. For him our project made more sense than that of the developer, and he agreed to do everything he could to help us get authorisation from the planning department. For me, this was clearly the green light from God.

But the problem of the staircase remained. As an engineer by training, and having worked for some time in the construction industry, I knew that this issue could be crippling for the whole project. A few weeks later I received the response from the town hall and, provided that we kept to a maximum capacity of fifteen people, we were not obliged to build an additional staircase. This was great news because such an addition would actually not have been technically feasible and we would have had to abandon the project.

Another point of coincidence struck me: when the Senior Pastor had bought the Christian Fraternity house some thirty years before, it had been a large house inhabited by an elderly single lady who had only used the top floor. The whole house required a lot of restoration work. The house now available to us was also inhabited by an elderly lady who only used the ground floor, and this house also needed a lot of and repair and renovation. It felt to me, that God was causing history to repeat itself a generation later.

Purchase negotiation and divine provision

The house was actually for sale with a second property, to be purchased separately, a barn and some land at the rear of the house. This part of the sale was not really of interest to Ellel France because the restoration of the barn would have required a lot of work for it to be of any use as guest accommodation. The trouble was that the sole condition imposed by the local planning department, in regard to the main house, was that we provide five parking spaces, one for each guest room. However, the only space available was on the ground being sold with the barn. The purchase of this barn and its land became another miracle of divine intervention.

Theorectically, we could have considered buying the barn for Ellel France, but we just didn't have the financial capability. On the other hand, we didn't want this part of the whole property to be bought by someone not connected with the Ministry, because of the close proximity between

the two buildings. We felt in our hearts that they should
not be not separated. Then the Lord spoke to a couple who
were on the team of Ellel France. They decided God was
encouraging them to purchase the barn and the land in
their own name, to develop this part of the property as a
house for themselves, and also to make ground available to
Ellel for the five parking spaces.

So we met the owner's agent to agree the purchase and
again we saw the hand of the Lord during the negotiations.
We were able to obtain the two parts of the property
together, resulting in a discounted price. We were
concerned not to put Ellel France in debt over this purchase
and by the grace of the Lord we ended up not needing
loans from a bank to finance the project. With advice from
a lawyer, five people involved in the Ellel France joined
together with Ellel in a special group called a Société Civile
Immobilière (SCI), specifically to provide funds for the
purchase of the house. As part of the arrangement, the
group members gave a loan, at 0% interest, to Ellel France,
sufficient for it to hold a 60% majority of shares in the
society, and therefore be the primary shareholder. It also
meant that the name of the SCI could be Ellel France, with
the aim of the scheme being that eventually Ellel France
would be the sole owner.

Throughout the restoration of the house, we have
continued to see the providence of God. With donations
and income received from the start of Ellel France, we were
able to finance the renovations, including new windows,
plumbing for showers, toilets and central heating, as well

as the decoration of the property. An electrician, who was involved in the Ministry, upgraded all the electrical systems in the house for just one third of the market price. By July 2013 we were also able to furnish the first floor and four of the renovated bedrooms. This allowed us to begin using the property as a guest house, in accordance with our commitment to the mayor's office.

My thought at the time was to close off the second floor and to wait for the necessary funds to come in but the Lord saw it differently. Two brothers from a partner church offered to complete all the work on the second floor on a voluntary basis and they even supplied the paint and materials for this purpose. We only had to buy the flooring. Meanwhile, another couple had also provided for the cost of repairing a kitchenette on the same floor and part of the furnishing for the bedrooms and dining room was done through donations of furniture. In addition, when we purchased the house, the previous owner had left us her furniture and we had been able to reuse some of these items, the rest being sold or given away where appropriate.

Through all this help, savings were made durng the restoration of the house to a value of over 30,000 Euros. By the end of April 2014 'The Refuge' was able to offer accommodation for fifteen people, in five bedrooms, together with a kitchenette and a dining room The ground floor was rented out to someone on the Ellel France team for private accommodation. Today, together with the house belonging to the Christian Fraternity and a little apartment belonging to the church, we have an overall accommodation capacity for 35 guests, not counting church and team members living in and watching over the buildings.

We thank the Lord for His amazing faithfulness over these years and particularly for His help in the completion of this special project for providing a place of welcome.

CHAPTER 7

Mending the nets

Recalling prophecy

When my wife and I were appointed and sent to be pastors at St Laurent du Pont in 1998, a prophetic word was given to us. This word mentioned that, after a period of fishing, we were then to be called to repair the nets. This seemed to confirm what we were expecting, simply that, having been used in the ministry of evangelism in the Grenoble church, we would be involved at St Laurent du Pont in new work, pastoring and restoration of the church in that town.

The Lord had also told us that in preparation we would receive the necessary tools and training to accomplish this new task. We also believed that we would then be training others to carry on the task with us.

The story of Peter the fisherman

The story of the apostle Peter provides rich material for teaching. This remarkable man of God was powerfully used in healing and the working of miracles, together with the important task of building the early church. Despite these giftings he demonstrated areas of inner weakness, even though he was very willing to leave everything when Jesus called him to be a follower.

> *Now as Jesus was walking by the Sea of Galilee, He saw two brothers, Simon who was called Peter, and Andrew his brother, casting a net into the sea; for they were fishermen. And He said to the, "Follow Me, and I will make you fishers of men." Immediately they left their nets and followed Him.*
>
> (Matthew 4:18-20)

Peter clearly had a call on his life, to be a fisher of men and an apostle, powerfully gifted in evangelism. But, although apparently full of self-confidence, he sometimes demonstrated a wavering character and a deep problem with fear. Quick to respond in difficult situations, he drew his sword and confronted the Roman soldiers in the Garden of Gethsemane, even cutting of the ear of Malchus. Jesus made it clear that He did not approve of this reactive nature in Peter.

> *Simon Peter then, having a sword, drew it and struck the high priest's slave, and cut off his right ear; and the slave's*

name was Malchus. So Jesus said to Peter, "Put the sword into the sheath; the cup which the Father has given Me, shall I not drink it?"

(John 18:10-11)

Interestingly, this same Peter, who had been so willing to fight the soldiers, showed some of the deeper fear that he carried within himself when servants outside the house of the high priest accused him of being a follower of Jesus.

Now Peter was sitting outside in the courtyard, and a servant girl came to him and said, "You too were with Jesus the Galilean." But he denied it before them all, saying, "I do not know what you are talking about."

(Matthew 26: 69-70)

We frequently see that Peter found it difficult to understand how Jesus wanted him to respond to situations:

From that time Jesus began to show His disciples that He must go to Jerusalem, and suffer many things from the elders and chief priests and scribes, and be killed, and be raised up on the third day. Peter took Him aside and began to rebuke Him, saying, "God forbid it, Lord! This shall never happen to You." But He turned and said to Peter, "Get behind Me, Satan! You are a stumbling block to Me; for you are not setting your mind on God's interests, but man's."

(Matthew 16: 21-23)

Jesus was sharing with His disciples God's call for Him to suffer and die for the salvation of humanity. Peter reacted from his carnal desire to fix the things Jesus was saying, but Jesus made it clear that Satan was being given a very unhelpful opportunity to speak through the voice of Peter, with the implication that Peter was going to need deliverance from this inroad of the enemy.

The first catch of fish

In Luke 5, we see Jesus teaching the crowds including Peter.

> *When He had finished speaking, He said to Simon, "Put out into the deep water and let down your nets for a catch." Simon answered and said, "Master, we worked hard all night and caught nothing, but I will do as You say and let down the nets." When they had done this, they enclosed a great quantity of fish, and their nets began to break."*
>
> (Luke 5:4-6)

Peter had been fishing all night but without success. Jesus told him to go and throw out the net again, and Peter made the choice to obey. In this passage of a miraculous catch, it is interesting to note that the quantity of fish was more than the nets could cope with, and they began to break. Peter was awestruck with what had happened and understood that he was face to face with the only One who could really see the sinfulness of his heart.

But when Simon Peter saw that, he fell down at Jesus' feet, saying, "Go away from Me Lord, for I am a sinful man!" For amazement had seized him and all his companions because of the catch of fish which they had taken.

(Luke 5:8-9)

In one way, we could certainly say that this huge catch of fish was surely a miracle bringing glory to God but, on the other hand, the breaking net would have meant a large quantity of fish were probably lost back into the sea. At the very least, there could be no more fishing that day until the nets were repaired.

The second catch of fish

There is a second story recorded in God's Word about fishing and the relationship between Peter and Jesus. It was some two years later, after Jesus had died on a cross and risen to life, facts that the disciples were still trying to understand. Peter had become discouraged and was finding it difficult to forgive himself for disowning Jesus. He sought a measure of comfort by returning to his previous job of catching fish, trying to push away the guilt, the sadness and the sense of failure that had invaded him.

Unfortunately, even the fishing was unsuccessful, with nothing caught all night. Suddenly a man spoke to them from the shore of the lake.

But when the day was now breaking, Jesus stood on the beach; yet the disciples did not know that it was Jesus. So Jesus said to them, "Children, you do not have any fish , do you?" They answered Him, "No." And He said to them, "Cast out the net on the right-hand side of the boat and you will find a catch." So they cast, and then they were not able to haul it in because of the great number of fish.

(John 21:4-6)

They eventually recognised that it was Jesus. For a second time, He instructed them to throw out the net again, which they did, and to their surprise it was filled with large fish. At the same time, Jesus was preparing the ground for Peter's healing,

So when they got out on land, they saw a charcoal fire already laid and fish placed on it, and bread.

(John 21:9)

Jesus was going to meet Peter near a wood-fire similar to the one he had been near when he had betrayed Jesus just a few days earlier.

After they had kindled a fire in the middle of the courtyard and had sat down together, Peter was sitting among them. And a servant-girl, seeing him as he sat in the firelight and looking intently at him, said, "This man was with Him too."

(Luke 22:55-56)

John chapter 21:11 has become a very important scripture for me, even though on the face of it it seems just a comforting fact concerning the fishing.

Simon Peter went up and drew the net to land, full of large fish, a hundred and fifty-three; and although there were so many, the net was not torn.

(John 21:11)

The writer of John's gospel chose to record a special detail here, and I believe the Holy Spirit revealed to me the significance of these words. It is surprising to see that, unlike the first miraculous catch, the net did not break under the weight of this second extraordinary haul of 153 large fish.

As I was meditating on this verse, I believe God clearly showed me the reason for this being recorded. Jesus was showing Peter, who was to be powerfully used by the Holy Spirit both on the day of Pentecost and in the early church, that he needed inner healing from the character weaknesses in his life. Without this he would not be able to fufil his destiny. Jesus did everything necessary to restore Peter inside, ready for his ministry. Jesus prepared the environment of a wood-fire and He challenged Peter strongly, but also with words of comfort, and he confirmed the calling on Peter's life. Jesus is using the situation to show us prophetically that a strong net, which is a healed church, the church of which Peter was to be the fore-runner, would be able to welcome in the large catch of fish without breaking. The net of a healed church today will be able to hold onto all the catch of souls that God has entrusted to us.

In reality, many souls come into our churches, hear the Gospel, respond favourably, go through water baptism and even Holy Spirit baptism, and then, despite all this, they leave the church after a few years. Why do they leave? For many, it is because they have not experienced the church being able to meet the deep healing needs in their lives.

New believers have come from being spiritual prisoners, but they are not then given the opportunity to fully discover the ministry of deliverance in Jesus. While still carrying heavy burdens they try to survive, but one day the inner distress becomes such that they leave the church and fall victim to the enemy's grip. It's not sufficient to simply say that these people were not truly reborn. The Word of God warns us that, as shepherds, we must take care of the flock which God has entrusted to us.

Those who are sickly you have not strengthened, the diseased you have not healed, the broken you have not bound up, the scattered you have not brought back, nor have you sought for the lost; but with force and with severity you have dominated them. They were scattered for lack of a shepherd, and they became food for every beast of the field and were scattered.

(Ezekiel 34: 4-5)

Jesus longs for the restoration of the Church so that it is ready to welcome new souls who inevitably come carrying their own damage and who need a shepherd to treat their wounds. The Body of Christ here on earth must fully represent the Good Shepherd.

> *"I will feed my flock and I will lead them to rest,"* declares
> *the Lord God. "I will seek the lost, bring back the scattered,*
> *bind up the broken and strengthen the sick."*
>
> (Ezekiel 34:15-16a)

A further revelation of the complementary ministries of evangelism and healing in building the Kingdom of God

Baptised with the Holy Spirit, Jesus was led into the wilderness where He was tempted by the Devil for forty days (Matthew 4:1-11). Despite Satan's attempts to deceive Him, Jesus gave no opportunity to this deceiver to take any authority over Him. Jesus remained, through every temptation, subject only to the will of His Father. After that He began to preach repentance and the coming of the Kingdom of God.

> *From that time Jesus began to preach, and to say, "Repent,*
> *for the kingdom of heaven is at hand."*
>
> (Matthew 4:17)

The importance of repentance and the manifestation of the Kingdom of God was the basis of His message. It is interesting to note that, from the start of His earthly ministry, Jesus was keen to surround Himself with a team. This is what we see in the rest of this passage narrated by the evangelist Matthew.

> *Now as Jesus was walking along the Sea of Galilee, He saw two brothers, Simon, who was called Peter, and Andrew his brother, <u>casting a net into the sea</u>, for they were fishermen. And He said to them, "Follow Me and I will make you fishers of men." Immediately they left their nets, and followed Him. Going on from there He saw two other brothers, James the son of Zebedee, and John his brother, in the boat with Zebedee their father, <u>mending their nets</u>, and He called them. Immediately they left the boat and their father and followed him.*
>
> (Matthew 4: 18-22)

Interestingly in the Gospel of Luke, in chapter 10, Jesus sends 70 disciples in pairs. We can surely assume that this principle of grouping the disciples was truly divine wisdom, so can the passage from Matthew, about the calling of disciples, give us more understanding on this strategy of Jesus?

First of all Jesus calls two brothers, Simon (Peter) and Andrew, who are casting a fishing net. Casting a net can be seen as equivalent to proclaiming the Gospel of Salvation, to fish in the sea of the world for the lost souls whom God deeply desires to save. We can say that, both symbolically and prophetically, this is what Peter and Andrew were doing. Indeed, the major role of the Church is to proclaim the Gospel to the world and this requires teams of apostles and evangelists who have a particular anointing for implementing strategies for the salvation of souls. Jesus later gave a prophetic word to Peter:

> *"I also say to you that you that you are Peter, and upon this rock I will build my church; and the gates of Hades shall not overpower it."*
>
> (Matthew 16:18)

The apostle Peter, who had an undeniable gift as an evangelist converting 3000 souls on the day of Pentecost, was to lead the early Church (the net) in a powerful work of evangelism and miraculous signs. It was the first essential step, but then Jesus calls two other brothers, James and John, sons of Zebedee, who were mending their nets. This call is also a prophetic picture: Jesus seeks balance in His team. If there are two brothers who throw the net, there are two other brothers mending the net. Mending the net, as we have seen, is a picture of restoration in the Church.

Two things should be noted:

1. People who have been saved by the Gospel message and enter a local church will have a need for restoration and healing due to their personal life experiences. They will be carrying with them the defilement that the enemy left in their lives before they came to know Jesus Christ.

2. The Church, because of her daily walk in a fallen world, gets injured and needs daily restoration. To deal with this, it's important for her to learn and practice the biblical principle of forgiveness, to understand the unconditional acceptance of God, and to seek for *agape-love* between one another.

For these two reasons it is necessary to have in the local church a net-repair ministry alongside the ministry evangelism; I believe this is what Jesus teaches us in this passage. Peter and John had different ministries, but complementary for the Kingdom of God.

Peter, sent to the Jews of his day with a powerful evangelistic message accompanied by miracles, had to be transformed by the Lord from a dangerously impulsive character (Matthew 14:28). He was also full of contradiction, sometimes presumptuous and sometimes deeply fearful, even to the point of denying Jesus three times. John showed signs of intolerance (Mark 9:38), vindictiveness (Luke 9:54) and worldly ambition (Mark 10:35-37), but he was called the beloved disciple, needing to learn the lesson in true love in the Lord's school. As a result, John went on to write the gospel considered by many to be the deepest and most spiritual book of the Bible.

Jesus had seen these two men in the true identity that God had planned for them from the foundation of the world, and not in the fallen and sinful nature that they presented.

Before I formed you in the womb I knew you, and before you were born I consecrated you; I have appointed you a prophet to the nations.

(Jeremiah 1:5)

When Jesus calls His first four co-workers, He shows a perfect balance in the choice of their profile: two to throw the net (ministry of evangelism) and two to mend the net (ministry of restoration and healing). For the Church to be effective in the Kingdom of God it must have the means to grow and the means to bring restoration and transformation to the people who make up the Body.

This is good and acceptable in the sight of God our Savior, who desires all men to be saved and come to the knowledge of the truth.

(1 Timothy 2:3-4)

Do not be conformed to this world, but be transformed by the renewing of your mind, so that you may prove what the will of God is, that which is good and acceptable and perfect.

(Romans 12:2)

Ellel's ministry is there to equip the Church in her mission of restoration and discipleship, to be gradually transformed into the perfect image of Christ.

*But we all, with unveiled face, beholding as in a mirror the
glory of the Lord, are being transform into the same image,
from glory to glory, just as from the Lord, the Spirit.*

(2 Corinthians 3:18)

Repairing the nets for the restoration of God's people

*The Spirit of the the Sovereign Lord is on me, because the
Lord has anointed me to preach good news to the poor.
He has sent me to bind up the brokenhearted, to proclaim
freedom for the captives and release from darkness for
the prisoners.*

(Isaiah 61:1) NIV

To repair the net is not just to announce the Good News
but to heal the brokenhearted. These are the people, for
example, who have experienced abuse in all kinds of ways,
those who have been traumatised by war, violence or
accidents, those who have had no parental covering, those
who have been abandoned by their family, and those who
have experienced extreme emotional distress.

To repair the net is also to bring deliverance to those
who have been imprisoned by the devil because of their
involvement, for example, in occult activity, in false
religions, in organisations such as Freemasonry, or through
inherited bondage from their ancestors. Delivering the
captives means removing the rights that the enemy has had
in people's lives and replacing these with the authority of

Jesus Christ in every area. Deliverance also means cleansing of land and buildings which have become defiled because of the sin of current or previous inhabitants.

The land which you are entering to possess is an unclean land with the uncleanness of the peoples of the lands, with their abominations which have have filled it from end to end and with their impurity.

(Ezra 9:11)

In fact the work of Ellel Ministries around the world, and not least in France, is, I believe, mending the nets. The Ministry is also training workers to repare nets, equipping the people in the local church, so that they can be ready to welcome all those whom the Lord will add to the Body of Christ on earth.

CHAPTER 8

Restoration and the healing ministry? Yes, but for what purpose?

The reality of the need for healing

As followers of Jesus, we should all be maturing spiritually, but we also know that, in the Body of Christ, there are different streams of thought or emphasis concerning spiritual issues. As I mentioned at the beginning of this book, I came from a very narrow non-charismatic background where we did not believe in divine healing and spiritual gifts. However, in this church environment I had the privilege of benefiting from a solid heritage of teaching from the Word of God. This gave me an important foundation of faith and I thank the Lord for the blessing that I received at that time.

Then I discovered, at the age of twenty-five, that Jesus still heals the sick and baptises in the Holy Spirit today. These personal experiences of healing and the baptism in the Holy Spirit, together with the manifestation of spiritual gifts, were a huge enrichment to my spiritual life. From that time I grew spiritually within this charismatic environment although, of course, I have also seen things that haven't been biblically right. I have come to believe that it is necessary not to be afraid of new directions in our spiritual walk, provided that we have the same attitude of the Christians in Berea.

> *The brothers immediately sent Paul and Silas by night to Berea, and when they arrived, they went into the synagogue of the Jews. Now these were more noble-minded than those in Thessalonica, for they received the word with eagerness, examining the Scriptures daily to see whether these things were so.*
>
> (Acts 17:10-11)

The deliverance and healing ministries are tools given today to the Church to prepare her for becoming like her Lord, who is returning to seek out His sanctified Church.

> *...that He might present to Himself the church in all her glory, having no spot or wrinkle, or any such thing; but that she would be holy and blameless.*
>
> (Ephesians 5:27)

Not everything in our lives is dealt with on the day of our conversion. As Peter Horrobin mentions in his teaching, there is a difference between the destination and the destiny in our lives. When I was converted and personally met

Jesus Christ, it was as if I changed trains: I got off the train driven by Satan (our adversary) whose destination is eternal punishment, and I chose to get on another train whose driver is Jesus Christ. This train will take me to heaven but, on this train, God has prepared works for me to do:

> *For we are His workmanship, created in Christ Jesus for good works, which God prepared beforehand so that we would walk in them.*
>
> (Ephesians 2:10)

These works, which were prepared by God, are in fact our destiny. The enemy who cannot steal the destination of salvation (by taking us onto his train), will try to rob us of our destiny, the good works that God has in store for us while on His train to heaven. The fact is that, for all Christians, there are areas in our lives where we don't have the freedom that God wants for us. Here's a text that has probably been one of the most misinterpreted in the Christian world.

> *If anyone is in Christ, he is a new creation. Things old ones have passed; behold, all things have become new.*
>
> (2 Corinthians 5:17)

Many have used this scripture to suppress all the difficulties that Christians have, and have given an interpretation that does not bring freedom to the children of God. They have said something like, "You are converted, born again and now you have no more problems. You must walk as if there are no more struggles, because all things have become new."

Let me ask you a question: a Christian who is addicted to pornography, can we say that his or her sexuality is under the authority of Jesus Christ? No, of course not. I do not believe it is the will of Jesus that this believer be dependent on pornography.

Can we say he or she was not born again? No, because if that person accepted Jesus Christ, the Bible clearly tells me that they are saved and the Spirit of God caused them to be born again:

> *Jesus answered, "Truly, truly, I say to you, unless one is born of water and the Spirit he cannot enter into the kingdom of God."*
>
> (John 3: 5)

> *For God so loved the world, that He gave His only begotten Son, that whoever believes in Him shall not perish, but have eternal life.*
>
> (John 3:16)

This person will need release in the area of their defiled sexuality and perhaps restoration of their God-given identity. We are created in the image of God and therefore with a tripartite nature (spirit, soul and body). This person probably has need of a deep healing in the soul and spirit, and perhaps needs to be delivered from unclean spirits. This sanctifying process and need for restoration does not mean that this person was not a Christian.

Now may the God of peace Himself sanctify you entirely; and may your spirit and soul and body be preserved complete,without blame at the coming of our Lord Jesus Christ.

(1 Thessalonians 5:23)

This person's addiction to pornography is both a wounding and a sinful behaviour but that does not alter their destination (heaven), although their destiny on this earth may be very negatively impacted. Imagine the damage that such an addiction can cause in marriage; it can even push it into divorce, with all the consequences on the whole family, not least children. The Evil One is a thief and he will do anything to steal what God has planned for our wellbeing. The purpose of the healing ministry is to bring the Christian back into their destiny.

Some while ago, I was invited to a conference in Toulouse, where several speakers shared on topics ranging from evangelism to the search for the Kingdom of God. I was asked to speak on the subject of inner healing and deliverance, and the Lord spoke to me in a very practical way, giving me a very easy picture to understand. Let me tell you briefly what I learned from Him that day.

I heard in my heart the Lord ask me a question: "How many mirrors do you have in your car?"

"Three," I replied.

"We are three," said the Lord, "The Father, the Son and the Holy Spirit! You need to know all three in order to really understand God's direction in your life; in fact, the more you know these three, the more your life's journey will be straight and safe.

"When you are about to overtake a slow-movng vehicle, what do you do?"

"I look in my mirrors," I said, "And especially the one on the left, here in France. It would be the one on the right if I was in England."

"Correct" the Lord replied, "When you look in the rear-view mirrors, it's to see if there is a vehicle behind that could affect your overtaking. This is like having a view of what God is doing when He helps you look at your life and He tells you about situations from the past that need healing through what Jesus did at the Cross. I want to heal each of My children from past wounds, some of which have opened a door to the enemy, who is holding them back every day from the fullness of their destiny. The healing I want to give them from past events is to bring an acceleration in their lives and their ministry today, to be a better father, a better mother, a better evangelist, a better pastor."

The Lord then asked me another question, "When you have overtaken the car, where are you looking then?"

"In front Lord," I answered, and then the Lord continued,

"When I act through My Spirit in healing and deliverance in a person's life, it is important for them to look ahead. I do not want them to spend time trying to dig up the past as this ends up just being a trap. They must keep moving and looking ahead, in order to continue to do the work I have prepared for them. However, if I had not healed them through the revealing work of the Holy Spirit, exposing the unresolved and debilitating issues of the past, they couldn't have have fully entered the destiny that I've prepared."

The healing ministry offered by Ellel Ministries

Here is one of the foundational texts for this Ministry:

> *But the crowds were aware of this and followed Him; and welcoming them, He began speaking to themabout the kingdom of God and curing those who had need of healing.*
>
> (Luke 9:11)

Here's another text that my wife and I received with regard to the healing ministry. It's about the miracle of the multiplication of the loaves and fishes :

> *"I feel compassion for the people because they have remained with Me now three days and have nothing to eat. If I send them away hungry to their homes, they will faint on the way; and some of them have come from a great distance." And His disciples answered Him, "Where will anyone be able to find enough breadhere in this desolate place to satisfy these people?" And He was asking them, "How many loves do you have?" And they said, "Seven." And He directed the people to **sit down on the ground**; and taking the seven loaves, He gave thanks and broke them,*

and started giving them to His disciples to serveto them,
and they served them to the people.

(Mark 8:2-6)

Here we see Jesus filled with compassion for a crowd of
people who are hungry and tired; this passage is, of course,
about hunger in a physical sense, but we can also apply it to
spiritual hunger, as Jesus often speaks of spiritual food:

Do not work for the food which perishes, but for the food
which endures to eternal life, which the Son of Man will
give you; on Him the Father, God, has set His seal.

(John 6:27)

What struck Valerie and me about this account of the
multiplication of the loaves is the fact that Jesus made the
exhausted crowd **sit down**. This was clearly important
in order for them receive the food that Jesus wanted
to distribute. Then Jesus gave his disciples the food for
them to hand to the hungry people. I suggest that it is the
same in Ellel centers. People come and we give them the
opportunity to reflect on their lives and then the whole Ellel
team, including those welcoming, teaching and praying,
is there to serve the guests in a comfortable environment
where people can relax (in effect sit down) and be able to
receive the liberating truths of the Word of God.

When the Lord sent me to Glyndley Manor to be trained
and given the tools to repair His net, I was new to the role
of pastor. Coming from a background as an evangelist in

our main church in Grenoble, I was accustomed to physical healing by the laying on of hands or by the exercise of spiritual gifts, but while I was in the Nine Week School (called the Flagship School today) the Lord drew my attention to a text from the Psalms:

> *And they cried out to the Lord in their trouble; He saved them out of their distresses.* **He sent His word and healed them,** *And delivered them from their destructions.*
>
> (Psalm 107: 19-20)

The Lord showed me that through Ellel Ministries He uses His word to to heal and it is His word that liberates, that sets people free.

> *And you will know the truth, and the truth will make you free.*
>
> (John 8:32)

Ellel's ministry is not psychological therapy. Very few prayer workers have any training in psychology, but we encourage each other to depend on the guidance of the Holy Spirit. Ellel's ministry is based on the Word of God and on the finished work of Jesus on the Cross, applied into the life of every person who comes to Him. Through the ministry we teach Christians to apply liberating biblical principles into their personal lives. Ellel's ministry helps people to become more attached to the Lord rather than to His servants, because there is sadly always a risk of people becoming dependent on man and not the Lord, which is a form of idolatry.

> Thus says the Lord, "Cursed is the man who trusts in mankind and makes flesh his strength, and whose heart turns away from the Lord. For he will be like a bush is the desert and will not see when prosperty comes, but will live in stoney wastes in the wilderness, a land of salt without inhabitant. Blessed is the man who trusts in the Lord, and whose trust is the Lord."
>
> (Jeremiah 17: 5-7)

Conclusion

My purpose in writing this book has been to explain the vision and birth of Ellel Ministries in France and to leave a written record for all those who will follow on in this work. It is a ministry that the Lord has established in many countries and it was His will to include France.

I believe the ministry of healing and deliverance is vital to the church of Jesus Christ in the nation of France and I have made a choice to commit a large part of my life to this calling, not only for the local church but for the worldwide Body of Christ.

I pray that the Lord will raise up many workers, particularly those equipped to pray, both in mainland France and throughout all French-speaking territories.

Epilogue

Taking advantage of this new English translation of the book, which was first published in France in 2009 and updated in 2015, we want to add some information on the recent evolution of Ellel France and some personal thoughts.

The continuing work of Ellel Ministries in France

Since 2014 the Lord has given us the opportunity to conduct healing retreats with a small trained team in a private home in Avignon in the south of France. In 2016 we also started a modular school in Roubaix, in the suburbs of Lille, in the north of France, and there too we have a team of volunteers using the venue and assistance of a local Baptist church: the pastor's wife at the church is part of the Ellel Associate Ministry Team.

In 2018 God led us to a church in the southwest of

France near Toulouse. This church, which had practised deliverance for many years, wanted to train its deliverance team using the teaching from Ellel Ministries. With the agreement of the leadership of this church, after two years of training (two weeks each year) we set up an Ellel outpost at their premises and today a prayer team hold healing retreats under the leadership of a couple representing Ellel Ministries.

The missionary call of Ellel France:

As a couple, we had the opportunity twenty-five years ago to visit Africa for training missions and to go to churches. In 2018, with the agreement of the Regional Director for Ellel in Africa (Derek Puffett), we got together a group of two hundred and fifty pastors from the apostolic churches of the Central African Republic (CAR). We were able to provide them with a ten-day school which was equivalent to Modular A series of Ellel Ministries.

Many of the pastors, who were enthusiastic about the teaching, wanted us to return and provide them with the equivalent of Modular B school. So, in preparation, three couples from the CAR came to St Laurent du Pont to follow the summer training which covered the Modular B topics. By God's grace, we returned in 2020 to teach this second school to 160 of the pastors who had already completed the Modular A training.

We were a team of eight teachers, some from France and some from Ellel in South Africa, and for 15 days we witnessed a great thirst for God in this nation. Today the pastors want Ellel Ministries to establish a centre in the Central African Republic. Sadly, as the country remains in civil war since 2013, we are waiting for the green light from God for this, but we believe that God has this precious country on His heart.

We would just like to leave with you the testimony of two pastors who joined the 2018 training; it took them seven days to travel to Bangui, the capital of the CAR where the training was held. While travelling, they unexpectedly came into contact with terrorists and the pastors were arrested and put in prison on suspicion of involvement with the terrorist organisation. God, by His grace, allowed them to be released and they were able to join the training.

Pastors like these risk their lives on a daily basis, and it's so humbling to see their thirst for God and his Word. May God bless them and may the teaching they receive through Ellel Ministries be a special blessing to this poor nation, which has a population of around five million people.

The future for Patrick and Valerie

We will gradually pass back the role of pastoring the church in St Laurent du Pont into the hands of the Lord and to a team of local leaders, so we can focus at least 80% of our time overseeing Ellel France and also the Ellel work in Europe. Patrick has been on the International Executive of Ellel Ministries since 2014 and David Cross, with the agreement of the whole Executive, has asked him (with the support of Valerie) to take over as Regional Director for Ellel Ministries in Western Europe. It is yet another step of destiny with which the Lord is challenging us, and we thank you in advance for your prayers.

Love and blessings

Patrick and Valerie

September 2021

Ellel Ministries
International

Our Vision

Ellel Ministries is a non-denominational Christian Mission Organization with a vision to resource and equip the Church by welcoming people, teaching them about the Kingdom of God and healing those in need (Luke 9:11).

Our Mission

Our mission is to fulfil the above vision throughout the world, as God opens the doors, in accordance with the Great Commission of Jesus and the calling of the Church to proclaim the Kingdom of God by preaching the good news, healing the broken-hearted and setting the captives free. We are, therefore, committed to evangelism, healing, deliverance, discipleship and training. The particular scriptures on which our mission is founded are Isaiah 61:1-7; Matthew 28:18-20; Luke 9:1-2; 9:11; Ephesians 4:12; 2 Timothy 2:2.

Our Basis of Faith

God is a Trinity. God the Father loves all people. God the Son, Jesus Christ, is Saviour and Healer, Lord and King. God the Holy Spirit indwells Christians and imparts the dynamic power by which they are enabled to continue Christ's ministry. The Bible is the divinely inspired authority in matters of faith, doctrine and conduct, and is the basis for teaching.

For details about the current worldwide activities of Ellel Ministries International please go to: www.ellel.uk

Ellel Ministries International
Ellel Grange
Ellel
Lancaster, LA2 0HN
United Kingdom
Tel (+44) (0)1524 751 651

Truth and Freedom Books

All available in eBook format from all the major eBook readers

Anger
How do you handle it?
Paul & Liz Griffin

Size: 5.5"x8.5"
Pages: 112
ISBN: 9781852404505

Hope & Healing for the Abused
Paul & Liz Griffin

Size: 5.5"x8.5"
Pages: 128
ISBN: 9781852404802

Intercession & Healing
Breaking through with God
Fiona Horrobin

Size: 5.5"x8.5"
Pages: 176
ISBN: 9781852405007

Soul Ties
The unseen bond in relationships
David Cross

Size: 5.5"x8.5"
Pages: 128
ISBN: 9781852404512

God's Covering
A place of healing
David Cross

Size: 5.5"x8.5"
Pages: 192
ISBN: 9781852404857

The Dangers of Alternative Ways to Healing
How to avoid new age deceptions
David Cross & John Berry

Size: 5.5"x8.5"
Pages: 176
ISBN: 9781852405373

Trapped by Control
How to find freedom
David Cross

Size: 5.5"x8.5"
Pages: 112
ISBN: 9781852405014

Rescue from Rejection
Finding Security in God's Loving Acceptance
Denise Cross

Size: 5.5"x8.5"
Pages: 160
ISBN: 9781852405380

Healing from the consequences of Accident, Shock and Trauma
Peter Horrobin

Size: 5.5"x8.5"
Pages: 168
ISBN: 9781852407438

Stepping Stones to the Father Heart of God
Margaret Silvester

Size: 5.5" x 8.5"
Pages: 176
ISBN: 9781852406233

www.sovereignworld.com

Sovereign World Ltd
Bringing together the Word & the Spirit

Please visit our online shop to browse our range of titles.
www.sovereignworld.com

Or write to us at:
info@sovereignworld.com

Sovereign world Ltd. Ellel Grange, Bay Horse,
Lancaster, LA2 0HN, United Kingdom

Most books are available in e-book format
and can be purchased online.

Would You Join With Us To Bless the Nations?

At the Sovereign World Trust, our mandate and passion is to send
books, like the one you've just read, to *faithful leaders who can
equip others* (2 Tim 2:2).

If you could donate a copy of this or other titles from Sovereign
World Ltd, you will be helping to supply much-needed resources
to Pastors and Leaders in many countries.

Contact us for more information on (+44)(0)1732 851150
or visit our website
www.sovereignworldtrust.org.uk